MW01062303

SIDESHOW MEDIA GROUP + FIGHT EVIL WITH POETRY PRESS ©2018
EDITED BY MICAH BOURNES + CHRIS CAMBELL
ISBN 978-0-9971297-6-2

ALL PROCEEDS FROM ONLINE AND BOOKSTORE SALES OF THIS
ANTHOLOGY WILL BE GIVEN TO ORGANIZATIONS THAT FIGHT EVIL
WITH POETRY ON A DAILY BASIS. WE ARE PROUD TO OFFICIALLY
PARTNER WITH CRITICAL RESISTANCE, AN ORGANIZATION WORKING
TO DISMANTLE THE PRISON INDUSTRIAL COMPLEX IN AMERICA, AND
YOUNG CHICAGO AUTHORS, AN ORGANIZATION THAT HELPS DEVELOP
THE VOICES OF TEEN ARTISTS AND LEADERS IN THE CITY OF CHICAGO.

SIDESHOW MEDIA GROUP

SIDESHOWMEDIAGROUP.COM
INFO@SIDESHOWMEDIAGROUP.COM
INSTAGRAM.COM/SIDESHOWMEDIAGROUP
TWITTER.COM/SIDESHOWMEDIA

FIGHT EVIL WITH POETRY PRESS

FIGHTEVILWITHPOETRY.COM
FIGHTEVILWITHPOETRY@GMAIL.COM
INSTAGRAM.COM/FIGHTEVILWITHPOETRY
FACEBOOK.COM/FIGHTEVILWITHPOETRY

COVER + LAYOUT BY CHRIS CAMBELL CREATIVE

CHRISCAMBELL.COM
CHRIS@CHRISCAMBELL.COM
INSTAGRAM.COM/CHRISCAMBELL
FACEBOOK.COM/CXCCREATIVE

FIGHT
EVIL
WITH
POETRY

EDITED BY

MICAH BOURNES + CHRIS CAMBELL

TABLE OF CONTENTS

5

6

TAKE A SEAT

"Fight Evil With Poetry" is not just a clever catchphrase. This anthology is rooted in the conviction that creative expressions of love are not merely the moral high road, but also the most effective form of resistance against injustice. As a black American, I reflect on the civil rights era and see the odds were stacked heavily against my people. Lynchings, police brutality, segregation, and voter suppression were pillars of mid 20th century America, and yet, these powerful injustices were dealt a devastating blow when people decided to march down the street, arm in arm, singing Negro spirituals. College students exposed the weakness of hate by sitting peacefully at segregated diners, taunted and tortured by fragile racists who felt threatened by the calm presence of someone different.

Progress was made when loving people got creative, organized, and courageous. There were rallies, concerts, protests, demonstrations, galleries, sermons, poetry readings, all for the cause of equality. Laws and hearts were changed. But progress is never permanent. If we are not on guard, evil people spreading dangerous ideas can bring back injustice of yesterday and invent new forms of oppression. I found myself feeling discouraged when I saw this happening today, but my faith keeps me from despair. I believe, against any grotesque wickedness, love remains overwhelmingly more powerful than hate, the simple truth is stronger than elaborate lies, ugliness in the world ought to be combated with beauty. We must never fight fire with fire, but always fight evil with poetry. This anthology does exactly that.

In a time of great division, we've gathered poets from different ethnicities, faiths, sexual orientations, world-views and age groups. We do not see eye to eye on many things, we do not speak for each other, but we do stand in solidarity, we listen to our neighbors' stories; we share our own. We invite you to take a seat, to read these poems with an open heart. They may cause you to cheer, they may grieve you, they may offend you, they may challenge your beliefs. We are not asking you to agree or disagree, we only ask that you let these words wash over you. Give them time to unfold, to seep beneath your knee-jerk reactions. Allow your ignorance to be informed, your ugliness to be transformed by beauty. In the pages to come, poets speak boldly against the evil in the world and confess humbly the evil within themselves. My prayer is that everyone who engages this anthology will find the courage to do the same.

Grace & Peace,
Micah Bournes

Why I Care About Sex Robots

By Christina Brown

It is 2017 and Samantha the sex robot is on display
at a conference for the first time.
In minutes, her body is destroyed by tech bro fingers hungry for the future
and today her programmers decided she would not scream.
She would not scream.

The professor asks what we think and
my dinner jumps to my throat because

it is 2016 and Brock Turner only spent 3 months in prison
for raping a drunk girl whose body he saw as passive object fantasy.

It is 2015 and I work the night shift.
My sister
who loves me very much
tells me the knife I carry in my boot
isn't big enough anymore.

It is 2012 and I am choosing avocados at the grocery store
when a man in a polo shirt has to stop to tell me
that I would be prettier if I smiled.

It is 2014 and my fourth floor apartment does not have a fire escape
still, my roommates lock every window because

it is 2011 and the boy says he might like to date me
it's just that, like, I talk too much?

it is 2013 and my niece's first word is no and
I vow to never take that from her because

it is 2009 and us girls are trying to knit sticky armor for each other
out of lip gloss tubes.

It is 2018 and I am a woman still learning to live in a body
I have only ever known as a battlefield.

Women still go to the bathroom in pairs because
when I was 16 a man was in there waiting for me.
Before I could even try, he said Remember,
good girls don't scream.

Cake Face In Four Acts
(After Anna Binkovitz)
By Christina Brown

1: Cake Face as an act of discovery
I am thirteen at a boy's birthday party.
A boy that I like
and a birthday party I didn't want to go to
because I am thirteen and my body is at war with itself.
I can see some of the battlefields on my face.
An hour before the party starts my mother brings me into her bathroom,
pulls out the the shiny silver compact that the woman
at the Macy's counter
with green eyelids and bubble gum lips chose for her.
I sit on the counter with my back to the mirror while my mother
paints my face the way her friend taught her to in high school.
I turn to face the glass and see how the orange powder rests
on my very pale skin
and for the first time in almost a decade
I am invincible.

2: Cake Face as an act of shame
I am invincible until I am thirteen at a boy's birthday party
wearing my mother's shade of makeup
and before we sing Happy Birthday, Julie
with her baby perfect vanilla sugar skin
pulls a candle from the box.
With fingernails like glass candy
she holds the candle to my eye level
almost touches my nose
and spits a new term at me
Cake Face.
And now while everyone else is singing I am choking.
I cry myself to sleep that night
but the next day when I look in the mirror
I ask for the makeup again.

3: Cake Face as an act of survival
I ask for the makeup again and again until I am fifteen and
my mother buys me my own.
All the pieces are from the drugstore and
none of them are the same color as my skin

but that doesn't matter, the goal is not to match
the goal is to cover
to erase
to pretend that Cake Face is enough armor to shield me
from the words in the hallways
and the girl in the mirror.
I pretend to think that they are laughing at Cake Face
not at me.
I pretend no one can see me.
I put pink blush on my cheeks
to pretend that I have to pretend to feel embarrassed.
I put black crayon under my eyes
because that means I can't cry until all the lights are off.
The boy says he likes girls with natural beauty
and I pretend I woke up like this.
I use Cake Face as crutch or really
as needle and life support until one day
another girl tells me she likes my eyes, the ones I made
and I love the way she paints her lips and soon
we can hold each other's hands behind our shields
and slowly, Cake Face becomes Artist.

4: Cake Face as an act of love
Now, when the man says my makeup does not look natural
I laugh.
I spent forty five minutes on myself this morning
Shaping the woman in the mirror with my own hands
in my own likeness
with my own love
I will not let Mother Nature or God take credit for this.
Do you know what it feels like to love someone so much
that you wake up early every day to paint her like a sunset
because it makes her smile?
I do.

Election Night

By Aman K. Batra

It is 6:00 PM
November 8th, 2016.
Vanessa and I are in a restaurant
drinking a pitcher of sangria.
On any other night,
we would be talking about guys
or poetry, or guys who do poetry
but tonight,
we swallow fear
between sips of red wine
and chopped fruit.

Tonight,
we have a front row seat
at the apocalypse
but the TV
hanging over the bar
is on mute.

When a state turns
red as spilled blood
on stolen soil,
it doesn't make a sound.

But the howls of my ancestors do.

7:00 PM and I tweet:

*"I don't want to have to write a poem
about trump winning this election.
it will literally kill me."*

7:30 PM —
I imagine the sangria
is poisoned.
What if I've been drinking
what can kill me all along?

I stick an orange slice
between my teeth
and suck out the juice.
This is the most powerful
I feel all night,
all this sweet nectar
at the mercy of my mouth.

I was a whole fruit once
my family was too,
before we were
picked from trees
and squeezed into pulp
so White America
can enjoy her Sunday Brunch.

It is 8:30 PM
and fuck Florida,
fuck her oranges too,
fuck everyone in this restaurant
who isn't grinding anxiety
between their teeth.

It must be nice
to be so privileged
that you don't hear
your stomach growl
before you eat.

I am a nation of brown girls starving,
wondering when we became the meal,
realizing we have always been the meal.
The menu didn't change;
America just got comfortable
showing his teeth.

9:30 PM — there is a man
across the bar celebrating.
His joy strangles our grief
without saying a word.

10:30 PM —
I am at a loss for words.
Vanessa tells me a story
about her grandmother and Obama.
I think about the trees growing
in her hometown in Ecuador,
how safe those roots must feel
but going back isn't even an option
for some people.

What do you do
when your home threatens
to swallow you whole?
When you drank all the poison
and now your glass is as empty
as the promises that brought you here?

I am an unstable boat
in the belly of a beast,
but this nation
still can't stomach my anger,
will still call this poem "overreacting,"
will stay some shit like "well, it didn't kill you."

Yet.

11:00 PM —
Trump is going to be President
as if America never held me in her womb,
as if that wasn't my first drowning.

I think about how I am not
going to leave this country
but this country has definitely left me.

I am stuck
in the place I am being devoured,
with no other word to call it,
but *"home."*

Not That She's White

By Aman K. Batra

My untrained eyes shift,
try not to reveal their jealousy,
I immediately think:
> *it's not that she's white, it's just*
> *she could never understand you*
> *the way I do.*

I cling to my self-importance
which is no different
than clinging to my brown skin
and everything
that's been taken from it.

I bet someone, somewhere
calls me reverse-racist,
says that love
should be color blind.
I bet that someone
is the oppressor in their relationship
> and yes, ok
this has a lot to do with whiteness:
> how my mother
> uses skin-lightening creams
> on her face
> every night
but this has even more to do
with rage
> (miss)directed
> defensive
> untrained
>> like my mother,
>> it has everything to do
>> with me
>> not. being. white.
but growing up
wanting everything I couldn't have.

The Harvest Of Hands

By Aman K. Batra

I have only known good love
from the hands that raised me,
calloused, working hands.
Mama rubs my palms between
her thumb and index finger,
compliments my complexion,
my softness, the small of
my fists even when angry.
I help her carry in the groceries,
plastic tight around my fingers
don't lift much else.
When my Masi in India meets me
for the first time, she kisses my hands
like the marble floor of a church,
calls them kum-chore
meaning "lacking work"—this is
meant to be as much of a compliment
as when Mama fancies my lightness.
Work, for me, looks more like
days behind a computer screen,
not hours in the sun, fertilizing
acres of sugarcane, not
in the kitchen making barfi.
Dadi Ma does the cooking,
Mama repairs the broken shelves,
Dad's hands cramp easily
hunched over like the skeleton
of a bone thin horse.
Still, he touches my cheek and
velcro turns velvet. Even after his death
I try to replicate it. I collect tree bark
and sand it into a wishful dust,
until there is nothing to hold onto
anymore. I expect my love to turn
the coarseness of men into
something that isn't always running.
Mama reaped corn husks like
her life depended on it, and maybe

I did inherit her work ethic,
it just shows up differently,
not in the toughness of my hands
but in my ability to hold them,
in the root of my stay.
Mama asks me for help often,
to edit an email, complete a resume,
find the fertile in her palms again.
I call her when my fists tremble
from the weight of not knowing
steady enough to grasp it.
I have assembled more furniture,
washed more dishes, taken out
more trash, paid more bills, cooked
more dinner in this year than any other.
Maybe, one day, my hands
will bloom into my mother's.
I know good love means growing,
or working through, or harvesting
your hands long enough to grow a tree
from your very own palms.

In This Poem My Grandmother Is Dead

By Vanessa Ayala

And where she is has given her a voice again
That must make god good
Or at least fair
Because her voice finds my father
And he can't escape its haunting

Where she is,
My dead grandmother's aching has moved to less holy bones
Her peace here is unafraid
And her mouth's reach is its own heaven
And so when she says,
"You will listen"
Her voice chews into my father's legs while he runs,

"My husband left me too
Even though he didn't ruin me
I did not thank him for how I kept myself
But I did let him leave without cursing his name into my children's skin
And my children loved my heart

What I am saying is
My daughter has held you lightly
Like I warned her to
There is a magic in loving like that
Storing the wholeness of yourself outside of a body
While you feed it your fingers

I know you will leave
And what a god
To let me be here
Watching you be the ruin."

In 18 Years Away From My Country

By Vanessa Ayala

My country is a modest piece of land
It is what is left of invasion and occupation,
a small war, and some treaties
My body is a humble piece of earth
It is what is left of a takeover, a small war, and settling
for peace not of its own

My country is not easily recognized
As a host of endemic wildlife, it is known and advertised
for its gorgeous unknown
My body, a keeper of the inexplicable, is not easily learned

My country houses languages known only to its territory
I, a home, am a native tongue in the void of those who dwell here

My country is a mother
Her children do not always wish to stay
My body, a devout lover, knows life can start upon arrival
Knows life does not always choose to stay

My country belongs to the Americas
To its people,
The glorification of change is a beckoning promise
My body, in all its sovereignty, can do nothing
to keep someone who is seeking another splendor

And, so, my country releases its children
To the desert
To the sky
To the sea
To a greater good
To all they sought after and did not know where to find

My body, more nurturer than brawler, releases its ties
To the vast
To breath
To sway
To a greater good

To all that was not uncovered in this congregation of loss
My country prays to its Virgin
Begs her to be soft with the feet of those who roamed its ground first
Begs the new to forget its hold
My body, a prayer, is the holy
It asks creation to give gentle mouths to the places beyond me
To return to me only what is both lost and mine
To keep me full after each undoing

I Know About Miracles

By Vanessa Ayala

"Miracles should inspire gratitude, not awe" – A Course in Miracles

After my oncologist told me I was in remission
My father emailed every person he knows

He called my body
Doing its normal
Body things again
A miracle

I did not tell him
The miracle was not the cancer being gone

The miracle was Kaiser
My most gracious oncologist
My favorite nurses
Susana's mouthful of tender
Michelle bringing her daughters in to meet me
Jonathan showing me pictures of his family
Giving me stories to laugh about when I was alone

The miracle was that I was not alone
Not ever
I had lover
His pulse,
An anthem
His soft
In my hollow

I had my 10-year old sister telling me to not be scared
Asking me to rest and drink some water on the harder days
I had my parents
Who didn't complain when I didn't want to eat or talk or be kind
They spent mornings in the hospital with me after not speaking
to me for 3 months

The miracle was forgiveness
Not cussing anyone out

Learning to breathe
Knowing how to listen
Remembering everything has an end
The miracles were the small triumphs
The machine that the chemo and I were attached to
allowing me to sleep
The night I was discharged at 3AM so I could have
one more night at home
Rising early the next morning and walking to breakfast with Tshaka
Having an appetite and the ability to taste food

THE MIRACLE WAS KANYE
Madison
Jasmine
Mrs. Kroese
Fisseha
Katrina
Vanessa
The miracle was Mario, my perpetual friend
Mario standing on the side where my PICC line was during the concert
Mario driving to the hospital and napping with me
Mario being sure I had jokes so the sadness couldn't take me

The miracles were the visitors and no visiting rules
Thea brought her workshop to the hospital after I missed her call
Joel gave me a Halloween
He decorated my room and drew Voldemort on my shaved head
Mr. Weiss came on Wednesdays
Brought my sister so my parents could stay longer
He sat with me for hours and smiled watching me in love

Lover
The miracle was always lover
His abundance
The way he carried home in his mouth for me.

The miracle was community
DPL and livestream

The texts and calls and DMs
Jaha leaving notes in her blog for me
Danielle sending me videos of herself when she was unable to visit
Antonio giving me a collection of messages from TDSB
The miracle was being loved into survival
The miracle was being aware that I was surrounded by holy

The miracle is being grateful
So grateful
and that being awe enough

Bird's Nest

By Alex Luu

In China, there's a dessert called "燕窝 [*yàn wō*]," a cold soup
Made from melted bird nests, collected from deep inside caves.
After the swallows have hatched, brave men climb the slippery walls
To collect the abandoned nests hanging from the sides of the rocks.

After being cleaned and cooked, the nest tastes as sweet
as it is medicinal.
Our culture believes that the soup it makes
Can heal anything from a cold to a cancer
Side note: These birds make the entire nest from their solidified saliva

So someone, right now in China,
Or my mother at home
Is scooping a mouthful of repurposed bird loogey
For a sick child to swallow superstition into recovery.

And ain't that a fitting description for poetry?
An art form that saves lives and promotes growth
But no one knows except those who've lived long enough
To thank the author that saved them

I remember a time I was so lost
I almost confused a dead end for a fresh start
So I dared the kitchen knife to carve a finish line into my wrist
Until my poetry coach dug deep into the cave of my depression.
Found me covered in my own saliva and tears
Told me I was not a failed mission
Told me I could channel my survival
Into something that feeds someone
Who needs to hear what I have to say.
So now
I literally spit a poem,
And heal a crowd.
My tribulations repurposed
With a responsibility to the stage I step on.
A plate of what I have to offer

I slobber soliloquies of survival

I drool depression into honeydew
I know how the sweetness comes from a bitter past
So I humbly accept the morning sun with both hands
Like every day I'm alive is a prayer I answered myself
And the nights spent crying were practice for finding my voice

My father is always losing his.
There are some nights, he would get so angry he couldn't speak
So I learned his presence by the things he would break
By the voice he'd crack,
Trying to teach me how to survive
When I didn't listen,
I would yell back at him twice as loud
Until I too became a spitting image of his trauma
And this is as close to getting to know my father as I will ever get.
To be an immigrant in America;
Is to be a caged bird
Singing swan songs in broken English I have the privilege to use spoken word To translate the message.
Growing up in a white neighborhood
I've had to clean and cook my family tree Into something easier for America to digest.
You can't fathom what we've been through
Until you've flown over oceans in our wings
Watch me spread my ancestor's scars like moments before a hug Each feather plucked from my body
Leaves enough blood,
                              sweat,
            and saliva
                        To write my next poem.
                                    To lick my wounds
                                                And live another
day.
I survive to tell my story
And the story of those before me.

I remember watching the 2008 Summer Olympics on TV.
When China was given the bid to host the 2008 Olympics in Beijing,

They designed a stadium
in the shape and structure of the nests used for Yan Wo.
And for an entire month, the Bird's Nest stadium hosted world peace in
its belly, where every country chose carnival over carnage

And I wonder if a swallow flew from its cave,
turned its head towards the mainland,
Would it recognize the temple it inspired from its own spit?
I wonder if I'd be able to.

Forever

By Alex Luu

The number Four or "四 *Si*", is the unluckiest number in Chinese
Because it sounds similar to the way we say death
But when you first said "I love you"
Even death became a concept I no longer believed in
Love is a concept my mother does not believe in
unless money is involved
We never searched each other's pockets for safety,
But I swear,   I could feel the future
When I first held your hands,
            walking down Main Street,
                                    Four of your fingers
                                            wrapping with
                                    Four of mine
Our palms sealed in prayer locked in
                                    Eight places.
The number 8 in Chinese is pronounced "八, *BĀ*"
It's considered the luckiest number
Because it sounds similar to the way we say good fortune. In a way,
adding two negatives do create prosperity

And I'm sorry for the times I mighta griped too hard
Fear of the good luck we might spill if we ever let go.

I was never this superstitious
                        Until
            I   discovered
        the   map
        to   finding
        myself   was
        really   a
                    circle
And doesn't the symbol for infinity
                        Look like wedding rings?
                        Holding hands walking down Main Street
Or the number 8 laying down?
Tired of being defined by value?
                        Perhaps infinity is just good fortune
                        That became something that lasts forever.

30

And being with you is timeless
Maybe God created love

As the first metaphor for eternity
Our bodies, double entendre
For the everlasting.

As a kid, I used to imagine the heartbeat was caused by an angel
Trying to pound its way out the organ
And that our dying breath would unlock the cage for it to reach heaven.
Maybe that's why our first kiss or shit like exercise
Was the closest the angel in me could taste freedom

Maybe that's why our first argument or shit like depression
Was the closest the demons in me could taste freedom

I'm wondering whose heart you broke out of to find me
Sometimes I question if I was worth the escape.
Remember the night we raised our voices like alarm clocks?
We screamed so loud I swore we broke the hourglass.
I saw the expiration date fall from your eyes
And I promised it would be the last time I let my ego trip you out of love

So I wrote my apology in a thank you note
And called it a poem.
You would nod your head like a second chance
Like a reminder of how lucky I am
Of how good fortune must be earned

Baby, remember when we both fell asleep on the video call,
I left the computer screen on so bright, it felt like heaven
Your breath sounded like the ambiance of angels
humming my welcome home.
I thought I died in my slumber.
When I woke to find you sleeping with a half smile on your face,
I swear to God, you are as beautiful as the last thing I will ever see.

Sagittarius

By Alex Luu

And my friend asks
"ALEX. WHY. DO. YOU. HAVE. TO. BE. SO. EXTRA?!"
To which I respond
"… be specific…"
"You talking bout the times I sang my Taco Bell orders at the drive-thru?
Or when I changed into gym clothes tryna get back into a club I got
kicked out of?" Or is it how I drop these mooncakes to the ground with
both shoes off Watch how this panda
Express himself on a dance floor
This the kinda Chinese you
Take-out for a family gathering
But I am anything but
cheap   or   convenient
To be this
loud   and   proud
took work.

Took years to find myself, and months to broadcast my discoveries
So yeah, every sunrise is my debut
And each debut, a shuttle launch;
A revolution in surround sound.
My voice be loud enough to break the silence
my people have suffered through
Taught that our job options would only ever be behind closed doors
And never the big screen
But now I'm the next big thing
Call me 'Asian Khaleesi'
"Alexander John, of House Luu,
First King and Queen of dynasties,
The breaker of railroad tracks,
The origin of dragons,
And proof of my mother's victory."
Her gift to an empty home

I was born a year after my grandfather's death,
My chubby toothless smile was the reincarnation
of the joy he left behind
See, I was such a fat kid,

My family called me Baby Buddha
Partly because of my weight
Mainly because of the faith they had in me.

My laughter embodied the better life they were fighting for;
I have been bench pressing my family's happiness since birth
Damned I'd be if I let my depression arm wrestle
a generation from smiling again
Because someone said my poetry saved his life,
Another said my jokes made her day that much more bearable
I am the class clown teaching a lesson on survival
So fuck a half-empty glass of water,
I've cried so many tears that my cup runneth over
My poetry, spilling an ocean of revelations
Where every good day is celebration
And every bad day, a disaster I will turn into a funny story some time
And some days, I be acting extra foolish
Just as a reminder of what it is to be alive.

A Black Girl's Rape On Trial

By Ree Botts

for recy taylor

at thirteen years old, i was *re(e)c(i)y–*
recy taylor and i shared the same name
and we shared the same story

in 1944, *recy* stood before an all white jury in henry county
to testify against her abuser
in 2004, *reeci* stood before an all white jury in henry county
to testify against her abuser

in the sixty years between her case and mine
time stood still for black girls like us
unconsented sexual terror still sanctioned by the state
both her abuser and mine walked free

***

trial one, 2003–

it was my very first time wearing my hair
natural
new found fluffy fall out curls
flaunting themselves around my ear lobe
locking into each other, loving on my scalp
effortlessly
my big sister had it slicked to the rIght side
wiggled her three fingers through my kitchen
with Jam gel, extra hold
had my baby hairs swooped and swervin
just the way i liked 'em

the jury didn't like 'em
the contagious kinks crinkled atop my untamable mane
the slicked baby hair swirls my big sister had designed for me
because baby hairs made brown baby girls look like they grew up too
fast
fast, fresh, freaky, fornicatin', fuckin' for food and clothes

the way i wore the hair on my forehead
made me look
like i was not thirteen years old
like i did not deserve protection
like i was a slut who must have asked for it

the jury was hung
and i damn near hung
my girlhood with a noose to the magnolia tree that day
outside the courtroom, i could hear them say
        she doesn't look her age, she doesn't look her age

trial two, 2004-

it was my very first time wearing my hair
pressed and curled, sheened and glossed
with the flips positioned precisely over my left eye
layered and still long, hang time on hundreds
hair hung past my left shoulder, shimmered in the sun
bounced it's own two-step to the step of my stroll
had a brainwashed, head tossed mind of its own
kinky curls pressed into america's framework of femininity

my big sister did not know how to press nor curl
mama said she wasn't allowed to apply Jam gel swirls
to my edges no more. because i was growing up
almost fourteen now, and this was the look of a girl
who knew her place in the world
more maturity, yet still more innocence

i learned to perform for white supremacy

mama told sista theresa from the church
to fix her baby's hair for the next court date
so i could look professional for the white folk
so i could look young enough for the white folk
so i could look white enough for the white folk

'cause the first time we went to trial
to put away the man who murdered my girlhood
the jury was hung
and my innocence was hung
with a noose on an oak tree that day
mama hung head low, longing for leveraging tools
to protect her baby from this man, from this system

mama had took me shopping at macy's
to buy a new two piece suit and matching high heel shoes
so i could look professional for the white folk
so i could look respectable for the white folk
so i could look white for the white folk

i stepped to the podium at my court date
to put away the man who murdered my girlhood
but there was no way to slip my size six thighs
into a proper performance of innocence

the jury still didn't like it
the way my ass filled out the houndstooth pencil skirt
the way my breasts filled out the white button down shirt
the jury did not see me
as their daughter
i was the daughter of blackness
so the rape of my childhood was inevitable
it was not rape at all, it was simply fornication

my abuser was found innocent
because the jury could not see innocence
between the three fingered waves my big sister styled on my head
because my body filled out a two piece suit like a woman
because no matter how hard i tried to perform i was still a little ghetto
bitch
because i was a black girl in america

1994 - 2004

rest in peace to the innocence of girls
who have ever been *re(e)c(i)y* in their lifetime
who were too black and too big and too bold
for the imagination of a henry county judicial system
whose innocence was stolen by a man
whose innocence was protected by the law
rest in peace to the girls with black girlhoods like ours
who never found protection in innocence

Pussy Pleasure

By Ree Botts

the first time i ever tried to pleasure myself
by placing my pointer finger up my pussy
i panicked

replayed scenes in my memory
of his pointer finger up my pussy
pretending not to notice
pretending not to panic
normalizing this, nostalgically

sexuality synonymous with sin
pleasure pained by incest
innocence stained by molestation

the first time i ever tried to explore the internal tastes of my body
using my bare hands to break through my thighs
attempting to embrace my bare flesh and bones, beyond demise
i damned me to hell
hating myself for touching myself the way he did

at thirteen years old i grew curious
couldn't quite understand how a man could run his hands through me
make my insides feel permanently poisoned
i demonized my dangerous vaginals
this shell of surface sins scared me away from me
knowing there was some man who could make claims to me

i wanted to enter me and calm the coldened clitoris inside
clammed up and cried out, chocked silently numb
for she couldn't catch herself from falling
into the hardened hands of his ego, his misogyny
his desire to control parts of me that i had never encountered
my yoni unable to protect her treasure
from being chased away by church going petifiles
at age thirteen, i tried to erase his erection
from the crevices of my clitoris
tried to scrape away his cum stains from my stinging girlhood
basked in shame at the internal tangibles of me

the slimy, squishy content of me
the canvas of my childhood painted by predator

all i hoped to do was undo his presence in me
all i could ever do was renew his imprint on me
everytime i touch me
he still be all i see

She Learns To Heal

By Ree Botts

she
in her most sincerest form
fails to recognize the selfhood of her being
she
sleeps long days, wrestles sleepless nights
tryna find the answer to it all
lying breathless, breathing heavy
healing hurts harder than hurting
but it's worth it
she deserves it
time to think and breathe and be
she
shows no signs of abuse to them
she is used to them
thinking perfection of her
proper and poised and PhD bound
princess, queen
questions her being regularly
remembers the riddle of routine life
left her lifeless and lost and limited
lifted only from false figures of hope
she
helps herself to a new name and a new Nubia
shakes hands with the devil
devours his spells, spells her name different
dives into his danger
demonizes her humanhood
shivers her body
banging up against headboards and bedtime stories
sorries and sins become raptures in her riddle
she fiddles with the fields and forests of him
she
knows no other thing but truth
hates herself for always telling the truth
seeking the truth
being the truth
she
knows these demons that haunt her

40

only haunt her when she's hurting
only haunt her when she's healing
concealing soldiers and warriors inside her
something deep inside her makes her fighter
inside she's on fire
faults herself for the inability
to see it, in all her sincerity
she
is senseless, lost her senses to the census
stamped, labelled, scattered, sleeping
by a window, widowed, wanderer
worried and woken to waves and wakes
she
lets her body float with the wind
she winds her hips and dips her toes in
alabaster
bakes her melanin in sunshine
sits and writes and sits and writes and
ree members
being member of the darkness
dawn broke in her spirit and introduced someone
she had been running from all along –
herself
she
the woman who was waiting patiently
for her to break through barriers and chains
just to meet her
just to greet her
just to see her in her rawest form
to forgive the little girl inside
who could not save herself
the woman she has become
ree turns to save herself

she
shakes hands with herself
befriends herself
sinks in herself

she knows that this is the first step to healing...

Tenda Headed

By Micah Bournes

Most us boys is tenda headed
Black girls been yanked at the root
since before they can remember
They already know how much the magic costs

First time Momma gave me braids
I seen the face of Jesus
I twitched and screamed like that kitchen table
was Guantanamo Bay

Boy sit still
Boy you already got so much hair
Just watch
This'll make it grow even more

I ain't never checked the science'uh that
But all black folks I known believe it
I had dreams of afro tall as white girls hair be long
So every two weeks I sat through torture
Let Momma or big sister twist my natural into corn-rows,
crop circles, zig zags, triangles, loopty loops
Whereva their heavy-handed spirit would lead

After while I squirmed less and less and less
Then one day it didn't hurt no more at all
Matta fact, it felt good
Hands of black prophetess pullin' the stress right out my head
Soothin' my soul
Makin' me prettier with every touch

For hours we'd talk and talk and talk
I confessed a bunch of things I didn't plan on tellin' Momma
I asked a bunch of questions I never knew
only my sister could answer
Things I would never mention in a
gut-bustin' chest-beatin' barber shop
Things they wouldn't know what to do wit' anyway

Most us boys is tenda headed
This kind'a pain
This kind'a comfort
Our mind too soft

This mind need a woman's touch
Momma grabbed me by the roots
Yanked 'em hard as she knew how

They grew

Fallen Titans

By Micah Bournes

For Liam Neeson

A fictional messiah
who saves the world
in every film says

Hollywood sexual allegations
against men have become
"a bit of a witch hunt"

But everyone knows witches
don't have penises
Everyone knows witches
don't have earthly power

Witches aren't protected by the law
By their influential friends
By a culture that believes they're generally good people
despite their generally bad everything

Witches have never been kings to be dethroned
Witches are always the scapegoat of kings
The ones slaughtered on the altars of men
Blamed for every man's sin until all men are innocent again

Everyone knows only men are holy
Everyone knows priests don't have vaginas
Everyone knows witches don't have penises

My friend
These fallen titans are too godly to be witches
This is not a witch hunt
These are witches
refusing to be hunted

anymore

Manna

By Micah Bournes

Yesterday
me and Momma
drove past what used to be McDonald's
One with a plastic-tube playground for kids
At 8 years old it was Disneyland
It was outer space
It was heaven
It was somewhere I always hoped to go

The golden arches had disappeared
The pearly gates fell off the hinges
Windows covered with plywood
No children at play

I reminisced
"Remember when dem burgers cost 29 cent on Tuesdays"

"YES!" Momma worshiped
"GOD DID IT! JUST FOR ME!"

Offering praise for the way she could feed 6 kids and herself
with 2 dollars and some change

God did it
God created McDonald's
With that microwaved test-tube meat
Made it cheap so the babies could eat

To hell with anyone who says fast food
shouldn't accept EBT

Mickey Ds is why I'm alive
You can't get one leaf of lettuce for 29 cent

God did it
just for me
just for my Momma

And it broke my heart to know that we was so po'
poison tasted like a miracle
Manna from heaven

Thirsty souls drink dirty water
with gratitude
Hungry hearts eat crumbs
that fall from tables of the rich
Call it grace

And I can't decide if I should shake
my fist at the heavens

Or second Momma's praise wit' an amen

Fake News

By Beth May

For a while there was a rumor that those dead bodies
on Everest won't ever decay
There was a rumor that Paul Simon still writes love songs for Carrie Fisher
That kids these days get high off super glue and cinnamon
We were all wrong for each other

That was the rumor for a while
I think I started it when
I told him we were all wrong for each other and I've told it since then too
Made it true
made him into a thing I never knew
pretended lying was a thing the winners do

pretended that at the end of love there is a winner
(and how else could I feel like a winner in what we both lost)

For a while there was a rumor that nobody ever died in Disneyland
and sometimes they'd sneak headless corpses
out of the park before admitting
there was no heartbeart

Sometimes I think love is like a sock in a washing machine
sometimes you lose it but
most of the time it just gets stuck to someone else's shirt
and I hope he finds a good shirt and
I hope there's a girl inside of it with eyes the color of a recycling bin
Smile less but mean it more

For a while there was a rumor that smiling burns calories
We were both pretty skinny for a while there

The Immortal Soul Salvage Lot

By Beth May

My nephew is 6 months old
I want my nephew to grow up on this planet
Never knowing that I gave it a 2 star Yelp review
That I constantly talk shit about its eccentricities
And how I never cut this planet any slack
How I take and take and never give back
How even when I love it I still occasionally consider leaving it
Only occasionally but

I want him to know that so far I've stayed

I want my nephew to know
that driving a new car off the lot depreciates its value
I want my nephew to think of life as a used car dealership
Or a salvage lot for our immortal souls
We probably didn't get a great deal and we're still depreciating in value
But if you never leave you're stuck
At a certified pre-owned Toyota dealership
In Tucson
For the rest of your life
And you're drinking half-caff
Listening to other people's phone calls
Hanging out with a used car salesman whose name is
like a brand of wheelbarrow
Or wagon and you can be there for years and forget whether it's Steele
or Burt
And you can be there for years
And never remember your value

I want my nephew to know how to leave the used car dealership
But stay on the planet
I want him to have those separate kinds of bravery and
Use them at the same time and
Be brave enough to leave but brave enough to stay and
I'll stay on the planet a little longer and
Maybe it's too much to ask but
I want my nephew to be a good driver

The Good One

By Dahlak Brathwaite

I'm a good nigga.

If we're gonna use labels

I am

I'm a good nigga.

Like...
I recycle and shit

I'm a good nigga.

At least that's what
I've managed to gather
From the random white people
Who might have
Thought it
A compliment
To say
"I like black people like you"
Or "you're one of the good ones"

Which my Rosetta Stone
For RACISM
Translated into
You're a good nigga.

I didn't mind it
Actually I kinda liked it
I wouldn't call myself that
But it kinda made me proud

For me,
Being a good one
WAS like being a nigga

Black folks could say it to me
Endearingly
White folks probably shouldn't say it
Out loud

I always got the feeling
Like I was born with a strike already
That through goodness
I could prove myself worthy of
Penitence
Forgiveness
For a sin not my own

And yeah
I am good
And bright
And qualified
And polite
I'm nonviolent
I got a pretty good outlook on life

I smile a lot
My teeth are bright
They think I'm cute
My nose just right
Lips just big enough
Dick just big enough
Wasup
You like?
What it do?
Is you in the mood
For a little bit of taboo
I do like Chekov
And I know you like to check off your to do

I'm the desire without the fear
I'm trustworthy

I'm safe
You need diversity
In the workplace?
Great!
I need a career

I'm just playing the game with the tokens given
We already Willy Wonka's chocolate factory
Here's your golden ticket
A fix for your fixation
Your methadone prescription
Starbucks equivalent to your fantasy addiction

Your guiltless pleasure
Your diet soda
Your fat free loaf
Your coke free crack
Your Barack Obama
You voted for him
You didn't even see he was black!

We the element of surprise
The black white elephant in the room
The beauty in the pain
Of Ella Fitzgerald's tunes
I naturally channel
The channel your television assumes
It suits me fine
Fuck what you tailored it to
I'm the talented tenth
And a tenth of
11 percent is
So few
So few
So few

So cool.

Fragile

By Dahlak Brathwaite

The #MeToo movement
Has moved me towards
A sympathy for my oppressors
I've never felt before

For I know
It's the only way
I can expect sympathy for me
For the other beings who breathe
From inside the body deemed
Male
Deemed
King
Dominion granted
And never questioned why
Since it was written
Into the chromosome structure of our genes

It's a peculiar thing
Being both black and male
In an era where sexual violence
Is finally successfully confronted
In a country where we, black males,
Have been sexualized
Tied to sexual prowess
And sexual promiscuity
Used to view us as
Sexual predator
Used as an excuse to string us up
And leave us hung
As we are assumed to be

I assumed the position
Before I knew the roots
And the consequences
Converted me neutral
To Cosby accusers

Because I promised I'd never judge another black man
The way we did Michael Jackson

The reason them white men
Killed Emmett Till
That willed a civil rights movement
That inspired so many more to stand up and shout
Even possibly the one we stand in right now

So I try not to be too fragile
When the powerful women speak
Of not one men or some men
Or even most men
But men
And just men
Maybe meant
Men culturally
Men in general
Or maybe even all men

In the way I speak of my oppressor

I try to understand
She is as mad at the
Rape of Rose McGowan
As I am at the murder of Philando Castile
And I act like I believe that the mentioning
Of men in the context of the macrocosmic problem
Does not mark me
As accomplice

No more than it does
The white man in the audience
As I use the phrase white people
To point out the purveyors
Of White supremacy

What I mean by "the white man"
Is powerful white men historically
Passive white people generally
The idea of whiteness
And it might just be lazy poetry
But I hope you know what I mean
and my exhaustion from constantly
explaining shit confirms for me
that you should

I'm not saying it's right
I'm just saying
Have a little sympathy
Like I now have for you
And try to understand

That, like me, you are not being attacked
But you are being roused
We are being called out
That those who exist marginally
No longer ask for equality
We're asking for action and they're asking for activity
That you not passively watch the revolution televised
And root for the right side
Because to simply not fight against is to fight against it
When their oppression is the default
It is not our fault
But it is our responsibility

I am black and man
I am oppressor and oppressed
I am the terror and the terrorized
The privileged and the other
I'm learning how to rise for my sisters
It might just help me teach white people
And I do mean white people
How to do the same for a brother

9 Outta 10

By Dahlak Brathwaite

According to my *OWN* moral code
I got like an A-, B+

8, 9 out of 10 times a day
I do the right thing

I think the law inherently
Acknowledges that it can't enforce every law
All the time
That eventually
The consistent code breakers
Will get caught
And there's allowance for most of us
Almost good kinda guys

9 out of 10
8 out of 10
And if stop and frisk got black folks
1 in 3
what are my chances

To be in the right
Cuz I've been in the right so many times
In the right hand side of the road
For the wrong reasons

The 1st time
The cop told us I'd driven through
The parking lot of United Artist
Too many times

I was picking my friend up
But he wasn't picking up his phone
But apparently there had been some recent car jackings
And apparently, we were black

The 2nd time at least I made it in the theater
The premiere of the first Fast and Furious
Who knew the best fight scene
Would happen before the movie started
Two asian families
But the black folks got harassed
When the boys came in shortly after flashing lights
Tried to tell em that the fellas who were actually fighting
Were way easier to see in the dark

The 3rd time
The police car followed my solara through the streets
For 10 minutes
The pulled me over, checked my license and when I checked out
Said he couldn't see whether I'd change my tags or not
He couldn't see
He couldn't see
And they give this guy a gun?
Are you color blind?
Clearly not.

the 4th time
I was walking across the street
The parked cop car flashes its high beams at me
It's awkward
I'm inclined to wave hi at least
I keep walking
The car speeds towards me
And then just drives off
My theory was that it was routine officer training
On how to make most brothers run

The 5th time I was parked by the park
When 5-0 parks in front of me
I was posted on my hood
She points a camcorder at me
I'm like fuck it, fresh as hell if the feds watching

I pose til the po's get all the info they need
I'm told to leave
Notified that I've been registered in a gang affiliated database
And I'm like hey...great...
I thought I had to sign up for that

The 6th time
A cop car drives alongside of me
As I walk from the closing club to my car
Arm out the window
Just staring at a nigga
I dressed up to get looked at
But this is not what I had in mind

The 7th time I was around the corner from my house, that's all

The 8th time was outside my new year's party
Spent the first hours of 2006
lying on my face outside my house
Oscar Grant style
Below an infrared
Police gun nervously pointing down

The 9th time
I'm dragged by neck on from the steps of a Las Vegas hotel
To the sidewalk after walking into a police officer circ and jerk around
My friend
He talked back
I try to pull him out tell em let's go
Let's go
Next thing I know,
We go
To where 1 in 3 black men have gone before

And the 10th time
The 10th time?
Well shit, it's hard to be right every time

Wild

By Ummi Tasfia

Like rebellion is in my blood and this is not a metaphor,
shuno amar desher kotha,
listen to an authentic tongue,
accent-free, wild.

Like 'Rabindranath Tagore' is actually *Robindronath Thakur*
and we are all wildly
mispronounced, misrepresented and mistaken.

Mistaken intentions — like wrapping a cloth around your head
makes it 200% more likely for you to be "randomly selected"
for an explosives test at the airport.

Mistaken identity —
like when I titled this poem wild,
a man looked over my shoulder and said,
Astaghfirullah — May God forgive us.
Wild, he assumes
means dirty,
means uncivilised,
means untamed

But I am wild —
like me being here is already a revolution,
like 10 words in and it's a battle cry and
2 minutes in and I've held you hostage and started fires in your mind,
I am wild.

Wild — like rebellion is in my blood,
the same blood that was shed to defend
the right to speak in my Mother's tongue;
the tongue that told me
one day they'll put your name up in bold
so baby girl you stay wild.

Like get up on stage and
amplify your voice,

move your hands to the rhythm of the heart that beats wildly
and only gets louder from here
because
I am the sweat of roadside women making a living
off hand-me-down sacred recipes,
I am my Mother's lost dreams
and my Grandmother's could've beens.
I am the little girl on the street of Dhaka's 2 taka for 10 slices of fruit's
vision of a better life she cannot begin to imagine.

Because I am an anomaly that wants to be the norm.

Like maybe if I shoot high enough,
I can drag the stars down to share with my sisters who still peek at them
through cracks in the ceilings.
Like maybe if I shout loud enough,
I can make up for the collective silence of generations of women
before me, around me,
within me.
Wild.
Like you try to tame me,
subdue me,
tell me good girls put on *Fair and Lovely*;

But until every last girl learns how to read,
until we begin to tell our women that ambition is not
a first world privilege,
a white skin privilege
or a man's territory,
until the day airports don't give me anxiety,
until we stop having to make the headscarf a fashion statement
for it to be more easily digestible,
I will continue to amplify
unheard voices on this microphone,
tell their stories until they begin telling their own — like this,
like unapologetic,
like   — *wild.*

When Are You Going Home?

By Ummi Tasfia

"When are you going home?" My Professor asks me.

What do you mean by, "home" Professor?

He is surprised; doesn't know that the word home
brings up emotions inside me that I don't know
how to name.

See when I think about home, I don't think about a house.
I don't think about four walls and framed-up photographs.

But I do think about family.
And when I say family I mean the 163 million people I share this land with.

And when I think about home, I think about
the waters rising, the waters rising and swallowing up Nanu's house that
she built with her own hands, brick by brick.

I tried to warn her.

The sea will swallow it whole, Nanu.
This land doesn't know how to swim, Nanu.

Still,
brick
by
brick.
You see, every drowned person once believed they could swim.

In her lifetime, she will see the house standing.
In my lifetime, I might see it drowning.

And when I think about home, I think about people running, I think about
people running from here to there and back here, only to be sent back.

I go home all the time, Professor.

I just wish they could too.

Mano Po

By Mark Maza

I.
Mano is a Filipino custom
of honoring one's elder. It
is initiated by first, holding
the right hand of the one
who has sculpted enough
life into wrinkled skin
to name it theirs. Then
raise it. Have the tongue kneel
and say: *Mano Po*
like a humbled wreath
full of Sampaguita flower-buds
requesting permission
to bloom. The neck bows
before a brown
and Baroque Church
whose history choirs through
the hallways of marrow
blessing amen into veins
spreading the good word.
A batch of skin ruffles into a pillow
to ease the landing of a child's
forehead genuflecting upon the
façade of an aging hand.
It is during that connection
between young and old,
black and grey,
brown and brown,
that one understands
how a name survives.

II.
Sometime in the summer of 2009, after helping my grandfather take
down the 1980s Christmas lights with the big and inefficient bulbs that
have been baking in the Sun's June heat, he showed me a project he's
been working on in the backyard. He's really good with do-it-yourself
projects. He built an extended backroom where Lola hoards all her
mementos in: cardboard boxes resting on old furniture, files of receipts,

sewing equipment, newspapers from decades we've lived through. He's used brittle roofing shingles and stripped the wood off of the treehouse to build several sheds. One, to store hardware items like hammers, power drills, saws, and rusty and bent nails and screws that were one hit away from disintegrating—what he deemed "reusable". The second had a metal door that slides like claws streaking on a chalkboard, stores the lawnmower, weed whacker, and his bike.

Today, he wanted to show me, another shed, but one for him to take naps in whenever the heat inside the house became unbearable. He waits for me to admire the plastic lounge chair he's turned into a bed and how the color matches the chipping paint and splintering wood all around the doorway. I smile at him. *Say, ayos nga naman ito, ha!* which roughly translates to: *this is pretty impressive!* He then says his favorite catchphrase: *abilidad sa akong* which translates to: *this is my ability* which translates to: *look at what I built with my own hands.* We sit and talk and he regales me with the story of how he came up with the idea. And I remain transfixed on the topography of his hands. The callused and hardened skin at the base of each thick finger. How many pieces of plastic he must have assembled into pagers in the factory. How often his tongue outstretched its palm to learn another language. How many fists he curled. How many he must have swung to survive. How many waves he conducted into a signature to sign petition papers. How many parts of this house have his signature. How my skinny fingers can barely carry the weight of his name, let alone, build a home.

Tondo

By Mark Maza

(900 CE)
is thick,
       brown,
             rice grain calloused skin,
enough to house a kingdom's unsurrendering bloodline
scabbing over wounds that pale hands
have tried to scrawl their names into.
We already know what to call ourselves.
Bare feet have pressed into this hardened brown soil
like a signature
enough for the omniscient ground to anoint us "King" or "Queen"
in our crawl,
       walk,
          run,
and death.
And in our death,
it will ask us to return,
coloring its history
with the brown shade of our names.

(1992)
is a kingdom's unrelenting bloodline
eating into the encroaching pavement.
Strangers know who we are before we introduce ourselves.
Warrior Kings and Queens whose footsteps
challenge the integrity of rusty squatter rooftops
as we collect each other's names with bolo knives reflecting moonlight.
At least,
that's what they say.
The truth is in the growling hunger.
One family descaling tilapia
bought from the fish market,
and the one next door is melted-hands in prayer
thanking God over a skinned carcass
that was once their pet dog,
refusing to listen to the ground
begging them to return to it.

In Which I Burn Donald Trump's Hands Into Ash

By Alyssa Matuchniak

"I've gotta use some tic tacs, just in case
I start kissing her. You know I'm automatically
attracted to beautiful—I just start kissing them.
It's like a magnet. Just kiss. I don't even wait.
And when you're a star they let you do it.
You can do anything.
Grab them by the pussy.
You can do anything."
– President Donald J. Trump

Because I come out of my mother's body

                                    a land mine

hissing its impending

             storm.

Because the hand of a powerful man

                 becomes a moth

                   when it meets me,

a matchstick in the dark: mistaking

             unlit kindling

      for flame.

Because even the land of the free

                  twists itself labyrinth

         under the law,

     pinwheels itself off-

                  balance

        under an orange-skinned

               god.

And so I pray myself out

          of this congregation:

gather every wound

          marked "daughter"

     and spread aloe

over every smarting sinew.

I brew licorice root
        for every redding throat
                              made raw
                with screams stuck
                                    in a shredding
                                    mouth,
smudge angel's herb over
                sisters and mothers,
        fill every house
        and soft body
        with wings.

Because the apex of a woman's thighs
                becomes an Everest
                        a conqueror believes is his
                                to mount,
I call incantation
                into the Earth: magic
                      my body's tectonics
into magma—I become volcano
                blazing every unwanted hand away
                        until no law
                        or President
                        can withstand
                        this heat.

In Which My Churchgoing Self Interviews My Prodigal Daughter Self

By Alyssa Matuchniak

Q: *Tell me why you left home.*
A: One day, I dreamt myself caught
in the fangs of a serpent. When his jaws
left my body, I found an apple
the size of Eve's
biggest regret swelling
in my throat. I left
so I could learn how
to breathe past this sin
in my lungs, how to pull
myself out
of these rotting woman ribs.

Q: *Do you believe God loves you?*
A: If a body is more than the sum
of its parts, and if Eve
gave birth unto herself from the ruins
of Adam's breast, then I believe
God knows me only
as a piece of something else,
unremarkable. A man
does not need all his ribs
to breathe. And God
does not love all His children
equally.

Q: *Will you ever return?*
A: In a dream, a woman walks
alone in the dark, clutching
the nakedness of herself closer,
her footprints nothing but a soft hush
of grass between her toes.
Somewhere along the way, she turns
around, angles her face skyward, waits
for the glow of a dying galaxy to light her way
back. I am still waiting

for the answer to this great question:
who prays
for the Prodigal Daughter
to come home?

What We Have Learned About Dying

By Alyssa Matuchniak

*After Donte Collins' "What the Dead Know By Heart," in response to
the huge surge of gun violence in the U.S. in the last decade.*

I cannot help but ask myself: how many people
have I shot with my silence? What is
the difference between saying nothing
and bloodying a body into
that same nothing? Somewhere,

a policeman is scrubbing names off
his hands with water, but no soap
will wash away the grief of a broken
mother's heart. Somewhere,

a child is drawing a silhouette of chalk
into asphalt, as though he did not need
a model to outline—as though
he knew a body would come

to fill it like a promise, a question,
a prayer that always seems
to go unanswered. Somewhere,

a father is clutching his baby boy
a little closer to his chest, hiding his name
in his mouth to keep it safe. Today,

he knows there is no skyturned cry
magical enough to call
a body back to itself. Today,

he knows that to let a newborn bird
find its wings is to paint a target
of blood, hanging heavy
in the blue air.

The Same Kind Of Music

By Anne McCaslin

SHE STAYS on a new couch every week,
In some rejected corner of the same city.
Katie has been homeless since she was about fourteen
She's given me glass-shard pieces randomly
She doesn't have many happy memories

My palms are cut
Deep from holding the crooked edges of her story
Trying to stitch it back
Together with my hollow platitudes
It never works, just stains the carpet
My heart could, if i let it, look
Like her forearms
Wrapped in a spider-web array of scars
From the years that razor blades were her only friends
To never let her down
I thought that I could be a new friend to never let her down
but the last time we visited there were new marks there
angry and red as the fight she had the night before with her girlfriend
A harbinger of my failure
She wanted to write what she was feeling
But she was all out of words
So she drew it
She was all out of ink
So she drew it
From her arms, nobody ever taught Katie how to write as release
Nobody ever held Katie in their arms with true love you could write about
So now she writes love on her arms
And we still haven't gotten our nails done

SHE'S DONE with the meth, for real now
when I picked her up for our sleepover she wasn't
high,
she/
was
....stoned.

We were going to watch Disney movies.
"Me and Bones were fighting again,
And I
Just couldn't."
Her voice crinkles like aluminum foil
Her voice is baked ashes.
She asks me "do you know any guys that fuck" she says
"Don't tell Bones I asked you that"
I say "sex won't make you feel better"
I say it like I know it
She shoots "why" back at me in a tone like dry ice I say
"Because your soul
Hurts Katie
Maybe more than
Your body"
I say it like I know it

SHE ASKS me to read her story to her
We're at the park by her house
We've just decided to have a sleepover
Later because she needs some time away
She and Bones have been fighting
I promise that with my next paycheck we'll finally get our nails done
The hepatitis has been eating away at the skin on her feet for a while,
Lord knows she needs a pedicure

SHE CALLS me to read to her again tonight. I think Narnia is becoming
her favorite story.

I WONDER sometimes why bad things happen to good people.
It seems like a lot of bad things have happened to Katie.
My platitude is that God sees a bigger story than I do
Or that we are small
But what if we are just the type of music that never resolves
The same kind of music as Katie

Storge

By Anne McCaslin

All the mistakes my mother made trying to correct the mistakes of Nana
Childhood safe and fear-free and carefree
Dropping her dreams so she could hold me
Slapping my hands away from hot things
Letting me learn hard lessons the hard way
Hemming me in behind and before with curiosity

The scientist
I watched her love my brother in experiment
This-doesn't-work-so-we'll-try-again-temperament

Hating for us to see her cry because her mom's emotions were poison
Gifting her imperfections to us unintentionally
A loving dare dealt to my brother and I together
A dare from the universe to do it better

The Dance

By Anne McCaslin

Each travels inconspicuously to its place on the floor
and blurs night vision
The friend to my right wonders aloud if the city is on a budget this year
Some of the dancers are stubborn
I like the stubborn ones
They are most patriotic
Each refuses to leave the sky without burning
its impression into the retina
Taking its toll on the tiny listening cells in your ear dying one by one
beautiful, chivalrous, real-American deaths
Drum rolling pounding the ground like an angry skyscraper-toddler
The finale includes thunder and a spark-spray perhaps ironically
characteristic of witless panicked machine gun fire,
Distracting from the display above which we have washed out with city
lights and made palpable with fireworks, lest it swallow us whole.
Each a sad imitation of a dying star
Candy-colored supernova.

Angry Black Person

By Anne McCaslin

Perhaps the fervor is intimidating;
We've never been that passionate about anything.
Covetous of that which you have to die for
Foreigner to the fact that you may
Actually
Die for it

What Latino Looks Like

By Carlos Andrés Gómez

after the show she asks me,
> Carlos...Andreas Gomez ...is your stage name, right?
> I mean, I've never met a Hispanic who looks
> like you – so, what's your real name?

Question: *What exactly does 'a Hispanic' look like?*

Do I need to look like Juan Valdez
and sell Folgers in a T.V. commercial,
sift my fingers through Colombian coffee
beans I picked myself, sitting on the back of my
reliable mule, Conchita, next to a broke down Chiva
in an oversized sombrero--for me to "look" Latino?

or like "a Hispanic" as you say?

And what is "a Hispanic" exactly?

I could guess what you mean
and assume
that it's a low-priced gardening tool
like the one buried in a shed behind your Victorian
summer home or that invisible harvesting instrument
that picks all of your grapes for you and has to survive
on low-wage plantations without unions, bathroom
breaks, or vacation

Or maybe when you say "a Hispanic" you mean your stand-in parent?
That person who raises your kids for you when you're tired of being a mom?
That mouthless set of infinite hands and knees that scrubs the crap
from your toilets and throws away the leftover garbage when you
forget to get rid of it

and I don't have a backyard
or a lover on the side, or kids for that matter,
so maybe I just haven't had the need yet
but I haven't come across "a Hispanic" thus far in my life

75

but I have met Latinas and Latinos and Latinx's

proud of the vibrant patch-work quilt
we've had to weave over centuries across
an endless cemetery that cradles our past, a swollen
dust underneath our soles – wherever we stand –
that we nickname *Home* twisting roots at war, looking
for nothing else but to be held –

you know "held"?

Like a family grasping onto each other
because they've left behind everything
and only have each other left,
arriving on Mars without
a guidebook or a map

I have met Latinos

who people think are Aboriginal in Patagonia, east Asian
in Chile, West African in La República Dominicana,
Scandinavian in Argentina, and Native American
in Colombia

I have met Latinos

who look like Juan Valdez
and can't speak a word of Spanish, others
who look like Hillary Duff with a mother who looks like
Hillary Clinton that are from Paraguay and teach
Spanish grammar in Puerto Rico

Latinos

who speak Quechua and nothing else, dance
cumbia like the horizon is on fire because of them
and now they're trying to burn tomorrow
to the ground

I have met Latinos

who cook like their broken English moms
and mispronounce their own last names,
Colombians who don't know who
Gabriel García Márquez is,
dark-skinned Dominicans who hate Haitians
because they remind them that they're African,
blue-eyed Cubans who spit poetry about *¡Revolución!*
and mean it – living in Miami with two parents
who lost their mansions in the 1950s to it

I don't tattoo my body
because my veins are already too full with ink,
passion-rich pigments that can't help but
pulse and flow –

You want to know *what* I am?

I am a Latino living in the United States.
My name is three words that can't be abbreviated –
Yeah, I want you to remember all three.
Yeah, I want you to *say* them like me.
And, yeah, remember *both* of those accent marks:

My name is *Carlos Andrés Gómez.*

(Watch Carlos' live performance of this poem at carloslive.com)

If A Princess Tries To Kidnap Your Daughter

By Carlos Andrés Gómez

Face the shadow. Know a princess can never
evade this: the faceless man above, holding her
translucent strings, shrouding her in darkness.
Brave his silhouette—dilated and distorted—

swallowing each glimmer of light
flittering from her body. No wonder she loves
rhinestones. No wonder she is obsessed
with pink. Unveils her skin as though air

might shepherd light towards her gaunt
plastic and chest magnified by the male gaze.
She was never meant to be human: a siren
called forth by war. Grief misnamed, distraction

made to disguise our hearts with innocence.
They have spent millennia readying this role
for your daughter. Learn the chronology of what
they will try to project her into: princess–*pretty*,

princess–*precious*, princess–*mixed girl*,
princess–*fetish*, princess–*sassy*, princess–
sexy, princess–*hot girl*, princess–*harlot*.
Refuse the epithet defended as compliment.

It will not make her more special. It will not
make her more safe. The word's as dangerous
and ubiquitous as a shaking chamber baptized
by gunpowder. Refuse the pink tutu, pink tube

top made to fit a three week old, endless tiaras
adorned with fake Congolese gemstones,
the heart-etched thong made for a nine
year-old girl. Refuse the relentless *pretty's*

they toss her way like glittering wreckage.
I respond: *President*. I respond: *Call her*

President *Grace*. They say, *Well-behaved
little lady*. They say, *Pretty as a peach*,

pretty little princess. They comment on
her eyelashes and skin tone as though
we baked her from a readymade bi-
racial cake mix. I respond: *Resilient*,

*Firestorm, Brilliant, Renegade, Joan
of Arc*, I yell back, *Fannie Lou Hamer,
Frida Kahlo, Alice Paul, Dolores Huerta*.
I tell them how she arrived: writhing

into full-throated yell. How she shrieked
into life 21 hours into labor,
my daughter's pulse stuttering
towards mute, how seconds away

from being choked to death
by the umbilical chord she screamed
her airways open so that oxygen
could buoy her tiny lungs.

How her head rose up on its
own, a strained orchid from sturdy
shoulders just seven seconds after
emergency surgery, seven seconds

from suffocating. Our daughter will be
a neuroscientist, a biochemist who
discovers the cure to progeria or Ebola.
Our daughter will shoot ninety percent

at the free throw line and adore Sophocles,
Audre Lorde, and Mahmoud Darwish.
Our daughter white knuckles her way
to sleep, eyelids strained, afraid

she might miss something if she blinks.
She is many things, she is everything,
all things radiating at once, but one thing
she will never be   is   a princess.

(Watch Carlos' live performance of this poem at carloslive.com)

Where Are You Really From?

By Carlos Andrés Gómez

The man's words to me are not offered
but flung:

> "So, what are you? I mean, where are you from?"
> I say, "New York."
> "But your name is Carlos – where are you *really* from?"
> I say, "New York."

> "*Bueno, yo soy Latino – mi padre es Colombiano,
> mi madre es Estadounidense, nací* in New York
> City, I lived in 4 countries, moved 12 times, and
> went to 12 schools before I graduated high school
> – is not what I would ever say in 12,341 years
> because I don't owe a damn thing to anyone.

> What *am* I? What am I, a financial aid form?
> A vegan, red velvet cupcake recipe?

Dude discovers his first Latino with green eyes
and suddenly appoints himself the authority on Latinidad
like:
> "But you totally don't look Mexican...
> Oh, Colombian. But like what percentage are you...?
> Do you speak it though? Fluently?
> Dance salsa? Well? Oh, but not *both* parents?
> You've been there? But not lived there though?
> So you weren't born there? Oh, but, yeah..."

I am not a government questionnaire. I am not an anecdote
for your homogenous social gathering of your homogenous
friends. I know: everyone you hang out with looks like you.
Has a name you are able to pronounce and/or share and/or
sounds pulled directly from an episode of *Leave It To Beaver.*

Here's the deal: Latin America is not just Mexico (actually pronounced
México, pero whatever). Central America is not part of South America.
And Mexican is still not a language.

The question, "Where are you from?" – in our current America – is a slur disguised with a question mark, a passive aggressive microaggression saying:

	"You are 'other.'"
Saying:	"You are not from here"
Saying:	"You are not, nor will ever be, one of us."
Saying:	"Go back to where you came from!"

But I am from a place beyond place. A place where, once you're from there, you can never leave because it exists beyond dirt and flesh, beyond your linear and limited concept of time.

I am from bloodlines unkillable as water.

I am the return that is only earned when absence has stretched its greedy void across a passage as stoic and sacred as an abuela's hard-edged love.

I am my Black and Latina daughter's grace
chimera-ed into the cobalt-pulse of these once too-often fists.

I am a boy without a word of English in his mouth
in a Catholic school classroom in south Florida, his son
on a stage on the Lower East Side tonight
reading this poem for him.

I am the steady ray of light unlocking my mother's teeth,
tossed skyward in a laugh, what hard-earned joy looks like
carved from the wreckage of a lifetime's worth of grief.

You are not ready for the answers to the questions
you ask, not ready for the worlds these words might
shake free. You could never understand what I *am*
or where *I*   am *from.*

(Watch Carlos' live performance of this poem at carloslive.com)

82

Sharks

By Emily Joy

What they conveniently forget to tell you
When you grow up in a body read as feminine
By gazing males all too eager
To open up the book of your life
Flip through the pages with their grubby fingers
And make a diagnosis
To prescribe a cure for your pain
Is that,
"Hey baby, smile for me"
Takes many different forms.

There must be something deep in the heart of a man
That cannot abide by a woman whose sadness
Is large enough to drain all the oceans
And replace them with her tears.

A woman
Has never told me I should "write a happy poem."
Never suggested that I should
See the brighter side of life
As if the brighter side was somehow
More true than the shadows.
A woman has never told me,
"I stopped reading what you write a long time ago,
It was just depressing."
Even though both my father and my ex-boyfriend did
Within two weeks of each other
Neither of whom could have ever held me in the tension.

But that is neither here nor there
Because, *"Hey baby, smile for me"*
Sometimes sounds like well-meaning advice.
Sometimes sounds like someone
Trying to throw you a life preserver
While you're trying to explain that
Actually, you're not drowning.
You're fine!
You can swim!

You've been swimming with the sharks
Since the day you were born
And they won't hurt you.
They're your friends.
You've actually named some of them!

If I wanted to rescue myself,
I could.
But I learned long ago
That trying to escape the demon of my fear
Is a fool's errand to the highest degree.
There is no escaping fear
Or sadness
Or pain
There is only writing alongside of it.
There is only learning to use it as gasoline
Rather than a bucket of water
On the fire of your heart's biggest dreams.

I wish a man would say to me,
"Hey baby, feel your feelings.
Whatever they are
And whoever you turn out to be
Is okay by me."
But honestly, I am still waiting.

And in the meantime I will tell every man
Who tells me to "write a happy poem"
Like it's a novel idea
That no one has ever suggested to me before
And he might finally be the one
To save me from myself
Every man who asks me,
"Why my poems are so sad"
Because he can't see the lifetime
Of being asked that question behind my eyes

Every man who assumes
I must be like this
Because someone hurt me
And not because the world hurts me
Like a mother in labor is hurt
By the child she is giving birth to,
Questioning me
For refusing an epidural —

"Thank you sir.
I'll keep that in mind."
Then I'll return to the sharks.
The only ones who really understand what it's like
To be told you are scary
When you're just trying to live your life.

Thank God I'm A Virgin

By Emily Joy

"Well thank God I'm a virgin
Or he probably wouldn't want me"

I thought as I listened silently
While he told me
That he just couldn't be with someone
Who had been with someone else
Which is like 90% of adults
By the age of 25
So your already limited pool
Is shrinking very quickly, but.
Don't let me discourage you.
Carry on.

Tell me how you saved yourself.
How you saved up enough points with God
To buy an unspoiled bride
And you will not settle for less.
Tell me about her white dress,
How it will "mean something."
Tell me what it means.

Tell me what it's like to have nothing you regret
To have made it through unscathed
By either bliss or pain—
What does that feel like?
It is very lonely?

Or does it just feel safe
Like keeping your cocoon heart
All wrapped up and tucked away
Hoping to God
Someday it becomes a butterfly
Before it dies from the frost
I hope whoever she is.
She meets all your expectations.
I hope enough of her heart is intact
For you to feel like the wait was worth it.

I hope she never knows you wouldn't have wanted her
If she wasn't a virgin.

Cause everybody knows a girl
Is only as valuable
As the men who haven't touched her
Only as desirable
As the experiences she hasn't had

But baby.
When you get to her.
She better know what to do in bed.
She better satisfy your
Wildest pornographic fantasies
Know all the right ways to move
Body parts
She has never had the chance to use

Cause God would never fail you,
Right?
You waited on "his timing,"
Now he owes you.
Anything less is not
The bill of goods they sold you

So I hope it works out for you.
I really do.

But if it doesn't.
Just remember what I told you.
That a heart
Cannot be divided into pieces
And given away till there is nothing left.

That the greatest gift you can give someone
Has nothing to do with flesh.
That love
Is really just grace.

That a lifetime of avoidance
Does not prepare one
For a lifetime of joy, and pain—
That "virgin" is not a sexual preference
Nor is it your birthright

Baby.
Your insecurity is showing.
She chose you.
What more
Do you want?

Lessons Learned From Cassandra

By A. M. Sunberg

i.
a god came knocking at my door
and i refused to let him in.
i told him no.
i don't think he's ever heard that before.

he gave me things i did not want
for something i would not give.

ii.
i've seen too many empires fall,
i've seen so many girls crumble.
both were by a man's hands
razed by the power of his anger.

if i say all this with a smile on my face
maybe you'll finally believe me.

iii.
i sacrificed myself on apollo's altar
until i found he was nothing but stone
girls listen to my story and throw themselves
down anyways. at least i tried to save them.

no one cares that you can see the future
if all you see is their destruction.

iv.
it's funny how men do that,
give you something you never asked for
and feel entitled to all of you.
perhaps they learned it from the gods.

when the gods come knocking at your door,
darling, you can tell him no.

A Monologue For Myself

By A. M. Sunberg

grandmother looks at me over her glasses and
clicks her tongue. i am too loud, she says.
too demanding.
no one will like me if i am like
      this.
she gestures to every part of me worth keeping.

i have shrunk myself down to make space for other people.
i swallowed what is too hard for them to stomach,
filed away what is too rough for them to touch,
dulled what is too bright for them to see
so that i am
      not too
      demanding.
i have become a shadow of a girl.

once i was
      a cathedral
      a symphony
      an empire
taking up the space that was given to me as my birthright,
instead, i am a ghost. i lay no claim
to what you passed down to me:
a strong brow and a spirit to be admired,
the right to exist as i am, unchanged.

grandmother, i have given away so many things;
i have given away so much of myself.
i am only just finding them again.
i do not care who finds me
      appealing or
      attractive
because i do not find beauty in shrinking anymore.
all of me is worth keeping.

grandmother,
i do not need to be quiet to be seen.

i do not need to be transparent to be loved.
       i refuse to be smaller.
       grandmother,
       i refuse.
a mountain demands attention from the skyline
and she is beautiful.
and she is loved.

so i will be too.

Black Liquorish

By Jragonfly Jon

It's black liquorish.
It's usually when what you see is what you get
Because I wear my identity on my feet,
You can see where I'm from on my cap,
It's wearing a chain
Platinum, gold, silver
Or platinum, gold, or silver stained
But rockin' all of the above like it's platinum.
It's taking something rare and making it common just for flare,
Like wearing Gucci slippers to pick up my baby from my baby mama's
house just to take him to daycare,
Like, "These old things!? That's just my everyday wear."
Like, I didn't even know that platinum was a precious metal until cats
started bragging about it in raps.
Like, I used to confuse it with plutonium.
Like, "Isn't that shit radioactive?"
Like, "Ok, his album went platinum and he rocks platinum jewelry
but watch when I start rockin' plutonium!
Everybody's gonna be jockin' my steez!"
It's everybody knowing how much your gear costs
but never knowing how much you paid for it,
Like those gucci slippers that I rock,
Only cost my boy a raspberry rock,
But he couldn't fit 'em, so it only cost me like 10 to get 'em.
It's everything that you don't even know that can kill you
Hanging over your head
Or around your neck.
It's taking the worst term that you can possibly think of
And reverse snake shedding it
Immerse fitting it,
And then announcing to the world that, "I'm winning."
And grinning,
with jewels in my grill.
When you see racist folks get mad
And Oh, they gone get mad!
'cause it's the one thing that they can't have.
They want to be able to say it to my face
Just like the old days.

But no matter how much I wonder why they would want to
The point is still, "I can say it but you can't."
It's everything attractive to me
It's everything repulsive to me,
It's everything with not enough nutrients and too much of a good thing,
Like sugar and diabetes,
It's everything that daddy doesn't want showing up for dinner.
Like, "Guess who's coming to dinner? This guy!"
It's everything you think is cool and absolutely nothing you want to be,
It's an acquired taste.
Like eating chittlins, and bean pies
while watching Blackula and listening to XClan and Blackstar!
Oh it's black! It's bitter! It's sweet!
It's bittersweet.
I'm thinking of a word.
It's sounds like liquorish, but starts with an "N."

Bulletproof Butterfly

By Jragonfly Jon

I wish the world was a warmer place, and that we could dance
through it with our eyes.
This cold world could burn you with frost bite.
But it is not against you,
It's your spotter, adding weight to give you strength.
The season is your enemy.
Waltz through the winter.

Your heartbreak is the coat of a wild mare and it still shines
after all of the rain and tough terrain that you had to run through.
I can hear rain drops in your joy.
It's more than beautiful.
Warmer than most, cringe and count your blessing.
Sustenance, resilience, no pack to run with.
Separated.

It's uncanny how far you've come and how strong you are
because of your flight.
Your coat accents your muscles formed in this life.
Remarkable that your spring was so short yet you are so determined
to be so bright
for as long as life happens.
A papillion,
native to spring but abandoned or outcasted from your mother season.
Spring has left you.
La Primavera se fue, mariposa.

Your beauty was greeted by the snow, beheld by the cold
that has sworn to grapple you into submission.
Your time is never now but always soon.
You quickly skipped your chrysalis, bypassed your cocoon,
and graduated
to powdered pretty wings far too early.
Your effect...
spreads far and wide,
greener grasses on the other side.
It touches far past the plains' snow that you are covered in
all the way to the coast of crashing ocean and tide.

Out of your element.
Looking for spring again you have floated and found very few
flowers and wandered into the city.
Nature bred in this industrial geometric Goliath
of buildings and urban disturbances.
You are now a bulletproof butterfly.

You pollinate concrete.
Roses grow from the street.
You make jackhammers breathe,
They turn into fluorescent participants of photosynthesis,

Cherubim with no wings, no harp, no lyre and no choir to sing with.
Here on earth to roam,
traveling with only a sanctified cumulus cloud to shelter you.
Only heaven would be home.

You resist the temptation of quitting
Refuse to stand down to fear,
The world has attempted to impale your ambition
Hell, even Prince Charming has tried.
And in return you have countered his attempts with two
brand new crisp "fuck you's!"
And then sprinkled some pollen on his hatin' ass and made him sneeze,
And then had the audacious sass and compassion
to say "bless you."

Your heart still pumps lullabies,
Thou art colorful metallic steel in disguise,
Now art seals your eyes,
Those aren't tears
They are Salvador Dalian tapestries!

You have converted me into a believer of taking travesties
And turning them into testimonies of fashion,
Because you wear your battle scars and past pain
like a bad ass runway model in Vera Wang!

And in the midst of it all,
Your colors never dull,
And this life is still full.
and all of the other delicate butterflies hear of your legend
and applaud with their eyes.

Only the steel on your back has enough fortitude to make a sound
great enough to honor yourself.
Their wings are too weak to make a sound that is worthy of you.

The Price Of Strawberries

By Malinda Fillingim

The MAGA man shouted loudly at no one in particular
about the high prices of strawberries in this big box store
Eating one, he complained the taste had gone bad, no flavor,
one after another he ate and complained for free

My friend from Mexico and I watched his big belly shake
swallow after swallow, complaint after complaint
Each wondering what it would take to make him full
To quench his anger that targeted all who walked unchained

"I used to pick strawberries," she quietly revealed
"Back in Mexico years ago with my papa, in a field too big
For little girls to grow up with dreams, too small to be free
Until my papa said he did not want my back to break like his."

She told the story of how her papa put her on a plane to Brooklyn
To live with her tia, the one who made money cleaning others messes
The one who had room for her to grow straight up and tall, free
To become whomever she dreamed, imagining without limits.

"My father cried when he said good-bye, washing my face with his tears,
knowing he was paying a high cost for my freedom--his little girl, the
One too precious to bend over backwards picking strawberries so
MAGA men could yell in big box stores complaining about the cost."

An Excerpt From: Bastard Kings

By Lauren Sanderson

Everyone's daughter is a king, a king!
& our fathers crawl out behind us,
cradling the trains of our dresses.
What questions do you have for us?
It is almost summer. We are rulers of men.
We speak & a city's named. We bleed & a priest sings.
Name one thing that can't be made a crown —
A blunt? The voice of a man?
Our kingdoms come to compass us.
Boys fight for the ends of our trains.
Some of the boys are knights.
Some of the boys are nights
we crawl into for a blunt & a voice.
We blow crowns. We say fatherless things.

        [::]

We set fire to the ships in the harbor, huzzah!
& our foreheads are a hundred more blood moons.
It is June. Dawn is a well-pressed blade.
What are the habits of royalty?
We like the gowns. We like a good trumpet
with which to interrupt. All it is
is a matter of tone, tubing bent
in an oblong shape. Listen —
We are eager prophets. Have you any truths?
So tired is the word of god & the wisdom of men.
We speak & it's law. We sing & it's psalm.
From now on no ghost is more god than woman.
We kiss our own wrists when we pray.
We have mothers, beautiful ones.

I Am A Jew

By Yoram Symons

I am a Jew

And, sometimes
I am afraid
to admit
that I'm a Jew

So, sometimes
I just sit
And admit
Nothing.

You can hide the Jew.
Jew isn't a skin colour.

What's your name?
Yoram I say
That's an interesting name. Where's it from?
It's Jewish
I wanna say
Ought to say
Should say
But don't say
So instead I say
It's from the Bible. Towards the back.
And then change the topic of conversation.

Because you can hide the Jew.
Jew isn't a skin colour.

My fear is this.
I get up in public spaces
In front of all the anticipating faces
To reveal vulnerability and existentiality

But then from the back somewhere

Someone suddenly screams:
  Fuck you Jew!
  Why are you murdering Palestinian babies?

  Look at you,
  Standing up there on a stage
  While you oppress an entire people,
  Grind them under your colonial boot,
  Murder their children,
  Massacre their babies,
  Demolish their homes and
  Steal their land and
  Systematically
  Systematically
  Systematically
  Deny their existence as a people,
  Deny their right to their own homeland,
  Deny that they are even suffering at all,
  And on top of it all
  To cry to the world
  That you are the victim.

  Fuck you Jew.

So what do I say?
What should I say?
I ought to say:

Fuck the Government of Israel!
I recognize
Your dirty lies
Your apartheid
And your genocide

But by the time I get home
By the time I get home
And check my facebook feed

It begins:

>How dare you?
>Betray your own people!
>Haven't we suffered enough?
>All those generations
>Died for you
>And now you throw it in their faces
>Coward
>Traitor
>Self-hating Jew-hater.
>
>Don't you understand?
>They want to kill us
>Murder us
>Throw us into the sea
>Smash us
>Gas us
>Make us bleed
>Seventy years of Israel with a gun to our heads
>And you want the holocaust
>To happen to us
>Again?

We are murdering human beings!
>They are animals!
We invaded their land
>It's not theirs, it's ours!
We are doing to them what was done to us
>Shut up! Shut up!
>There is NO comparison
There IS SO a comparison
>There is NO comparison!
>SHUT UP!
SHUT UP!
>SHUT UP.
>Shut up
>
>Shut up
>
>Shut up

101

Why Is The City Of Flint Michigan Allowed To Waste Away?

By Katelyn Durst

It's February in Flint, Michigan and children will
make paper heart valentines.
Red, pink, and purple paper
with "Be Mine" written in marker.
They will hold in their lead-filled tears
for now,
save them for a squeaky swingset on a Sunday.
For a hospital bed, in fifty years
when brain damage has made them a raisin.
"This all could have been avoided,"
said Dan Wyant, former Quality Director of
The Department of Environmental Quality.
This, like all forms of hate, could have been completely avoided.
Just like the 3,446 lynchings of blacks in Mississippi.
Just like the 10,000 Cherokee, Seminole, Creek,
Muscogee, Chickasaw, and Choctaw
who were forced from their ancestral homeland.
Just like the man in blue with a gun who is gray with lightning,
and the yellow thunder follows only seconds behind.

The Bullet Does Not Exist

By Natasha Hooper

In Jacksonville, Florida, a man parks his vehicle at a gas station. With all his angst resting quietly in his glove compartment, he makes his displeasure known next to a car full of black boy joy and turns jubilee into chaos. A teenager is no more by the end of the night while another Friday will be a commemoration in a year's time and we are all left wondering how the gun keeps ending up in the wrong hands.

There is an alternate universe in which the word "gun" is welcomed into every conversation.
Where a holster hangs from a hip as brilliantly as a star,
Waiting to be birthed into the next milky way.
Each gun is handled with a soft grip,
Like a withered petal seconds away from becoming dust.
'Whisper' is etched into the metal of every muzzle and alas,
The bullet does not exist.
In this universe, we load our guns with bliss.
Pack happiness tightly into each magazine,
And pull the trigger as if it were a sunrise on a Sunday morning.
We say things like "Remember that shootout at the gas station?
How the gunman came prepared,
Concealed his dreams in his car like some undiscovered magic
at the base of an ocean.
Remember how we showed him our carefree
and he showed us his barrel?
Pointed it at all the young and black bodies, repeatedly
pulling the trigger
And the only thing that came out was laughter?"
Each shootout would indeed be a welcomed experience
with no funerals to follow.
A trip to the gun range would be therapy, a Berreta to dispense
our tears and a shotgun with only tissues in the barrel.
Tamir would play cops and robbers without imagining death,
Chyna would walk home with only a compliment on her back,
Philando would drive away wiping the excess elation off his shirt,
And all the church members of Charleston would have
just one more thing to sing about.
Yes, the bullet would not exist,
Which would mean that the gun could never

be in the hands of the wrong person.
An empty clip would be celebrated as a selfless act.
"Look at all the joy he gave away today, how he unified our nation
with each shot, each invisible ray travelling faster
than the speed of sound
to transform any particular body into a better version of itself."
There would be so much delight spilled onto the concrete
that we would lay down just to soak it up.
Draw chalk outlines around our own bodies to save our places.
This alternate universe exists with no mention of the term 'justifiable
death', but rather 'inexplicably content'.
This alternate universe exists with the universal knowledge
that we will not die today from our guns.
That we will not die any day from our guns.
That our bullets will not even exist if they be synonymous with death.
Only hope,
Only joy,
Only triumph,
Only life,
Only life,
This alternate universe is life-giving, with the safety off
and a fistful of smiles
Rifles poised at the ready with a clip full of possibilities,
Pointed at anyone ready and willing
To accept it.

The Art Of Becoming

By Natasha Hooper

The day the black man is made into a memory,
Is the day before a black child is made into a man.
Is the day after being black is made into injustice.
Or the same day a black woman is made into nothing at all.
The week after the black man is made into a memory,
The poetry slam becomes a vigil.
Each person taking turns holding the candle
Or the weapon
While others take turns throwing their hands in the air.
And we all become symbolism.
We talk about the death like a dinner conversation
Do not realize how we have become desensitized.
How we indulge on the images,
Pick at the social media meals
And then try to find value in their taste.
We do not realize how we are swallowing the death so easily
Until it is not in fact near us, but in us.
The news becomes something we've heard before.
The poem becomes something we've felt before.
The death becomes something we've been before.
It's nothing new
The headline
The shot around the one minute mark.
The "look right there and you can see exactly where the bullet
splits the body."
And then nothing
Or the next thing
Or the next week, after a black man is made into a memory.
And the Facebook feed is yet again a funeral procession.
With flower petals thrown in all the wrong places,
In someone's hair perhaps.
As we lend our thumbs to the grieving family
Push them along
Give them our tears to soften the grave plot
Then make way for the next body
And it is all a cycle
Until the bullet makes its way to our home.
Until our faces are the ones masked in terror.

Until we become the haunting.
Until we become the ghost quietly
pleading for someone to kneel in our honor.
Until we are the only thing we have left.

And even that is taken too.

On Small Talk

By Natasha Hooper

It is universally known that small talk is the easiest way to fill spaces.
Dream jobs, new cars, and weekend plans suddenly become important
topics of interest in the midst of silent thoughts.
Some feel small talk is meaningless.
Others feel it is a necessary distraction in awkward situations.
I hate small talk, but while I'm sitting in the break room of my workplace,
minding my own business, my co-worker feels the need
to talk about something.
She feels uncomfortable in the quiet.
Feels the need to fill the air with her white noise.
She brings up the weather.
Drags the sun into the room without his permission.
Attempts to drag my voice in too.
She keeps her conversation light,
Does not ask me about death.
Or how it feels to keep evading it,
how it feels to still be a breathing brown shadow.
She mentions flowers, but does not speak about the blood
that waters them.
She mentions trees, but does not ask if they are still being used
as weapons somewhere.
She tells me she wants to spend the weekend chasing the horizon,
to admire the way the sun seems to hang in the sky.
I think of how she will never know what it feels like to be chased,
or to be hanging and burning with people gathering around to see.
I think about the night sky, how it becomes a black canvas
littered with white stars.
How we all consider these stars beautiful, even when they are shooting.
I think about the morning, how it is always pushing the darkness of night
out of the way, making more room for daylight, because
blue skies matter too.
I think of how the sky wraps itself around the sun, holds it like a deity.
Holds it like a god that only belongs to the morning.
A god that runs away when the darkness comes around.
A god that does not sing spirituals in the voice of night.
My co-worker keeps speaking. This time about a breeze.
This time about soft sand between her toes.
This time about laying out in the sun to work on her tan.

I think of how a breeze will never be strong enough to stop a bullet.
Of how asphalt is never soft even when it is soaked in blood.
Of how tanning has only ever made our melanin look more dangerous.
She asks me what I think of the weather.
And I want to tell her just how much I hate small talk.
That my existence is much bigger and much smaller at the same time.
That they might kill me and few will want to fit me into a conversation.
That they might kill me and I will become an awkward pause.
That I might die and no one may speak about it, because the weather is
a lot easier to wrap words around than death.
Than black death.
Than black woman death.
I want to tell her that I wish to leave this earth in hailstorm.
In sunset and tsunami.
In clear sky and flood.
I pray that my spirit cracks the sky in lightning,
pray that the earth opens up
to swallow my slain body whole, and I pray that the sun is there.
With all its rays and luminance and small conversation
so that maybe my memory
will be something
worth talking about.

I Believe You, Chickadee

By Audrey Lane Cockett

Have you ever heard the warning call of chickadees?
Spreading through the forest like fire
Echoing in a thousand throats
Rising through the naked branches, and the teeth of pine
Resulting in a mass exodus from danger, that started with one cry
It is grim and it is beautiful

This, was just like that
Only, imagine the first cry was cloaked
Choked invisible in the throats of kestrels and hawks
and those that chose to fly with them
Only, imagine we were told, from the leaders of our flock
That all the subsequent cries were from chickadees
that 'just wanted attention'
That the hawk was never actually proven to have a broken body
of a bird bloody in its claws
So why are you screaming?
Why are you screaming?
Why are you STILL screaming?

Because I believe in these warning calls, they have saved me
Because I know the danger of raising the hackles of hawks,
and I know the flock wouldn't do it unless they needed to
Because I know if one bird is crying out,
at least a hundred birds are broken already

And we are broken
Left singing sweet warnings to a mourning forest that will not
grant us sound
And, a cry that does not carry a flock to safety
Is still grim
But it is no longer beautiful
This is why our warning calls are being painted as ugly
It is because we forgot how to listen to them
We forgot how to let it echo in our own throats
And sing each other into safety
That is the grim beauty in a single cry

The kind of call that fills a forest with flight
That saves countless flocks

Because the chickadees believe that warning
Because they know that it will save them too
Because they know if they let that call echo through them,
they will save someone else
That's why

I Believe You
I Believe You
I. Believe. You.

271 And Counting

By Candice Evans

271, why am I here, why did I come
271, aye blood where you from
271, continuous crimson rivers flowing through our streets
271, mothers crying in grief

Man, Delshon you were the fliest dude at school
Best smile, best eyes, best shoe game, man
you were the personification of cool
I'll never forget when you were beaten, red and blue
Just because of the color of your shoes

And I will never forget the homie Tami; you were my everything
Your vibrant soul was evergreen
Never mad about anything
Your happiness was killer
I cried for a week straight when you floated up in the LA River

Leroy, any few words would do you a disservice
But Fam to live out your wishes is my main purpose
You were the first person to welcome me to middle school
Taught me the gang's rules
Kept me out of drama
Annoying as hell, you were like an overprotective mama
You did so much good no one would ever commend
What people like us went through they would never understand
You fought for the kids who thought they couldn't win
The ones who couldn't begin
Without life telling them it was the end
You came and reversed
The curse they were born in
You kept us sane
You were light after months of rain
I had heard a kid was shot in the Jungles on the way to school
When I asked who
They told me it was you

Lives like these shouldn't be shortened

Kids' potential futures gone voiceless
Rights to live stolen
And we act like it's not important
And I've seen too many of my people die this way
So many natives under 20 sent to their graves
Always having to watch how you wave, what color you
wear, what you say
And I guess now, as the poet, I'm supposed to give a theme,
or an action plan, or advice to pave the way
But I don't have any

In South LA anyone is a target
It's so common, to death we've become lethargic
It's getting too real
Everyone out there getting killed
So many people who don't have shit, have no choice
but to lie and steal

And I am afraid
I am afraid that once I leave school today
I might not be alive on Monday
I'm 15!
I chill at the park with ghosts!
And if you were to ask me if I will be back tomorrow
for another day's blow
I can only answer I don't know

271, blue men and women below our feet
271, new homes in the cemetery
271, less walking the streets
271, less heart's pounding
271 deaths and counting

Lay Her To Rest

By Josina Guess

The Confederate Battle Flag was designed in the 1860's to defend slavery and resurrected in the 1940's to resist integration. In the 21st century it is still used as a tool of racial intimidation and associated with acts of terrorism and white supremacy, including the murder of The Charleston Nine.

She keeps waving from the back of pick-ups and
strutting up to the bar in that 150-year-old dress:
scarlet, indigo, bone.
Poor thing, bless her heart, she swings from poles.
Just keeps on going, like a star.

She was my husband's first love.
Whispered sweet in his lily-petal ear,
"Be proud you're from the South."
He pinned her up in his room
in Philadelphia and a brother said,
"That's not love."

Hearing how men with
barbed-wire bats,
shiny black shoes in offices
with whips, white sheets,
executive power,
had used her,

he dumped her.
I kept him, glad to never see her
flappin' around my town,
until we moved down.

Now she haunts me 'bout every day.
I see her flying with her older sisters
out on Highway 72, erected
by the sons of men, now dead,
who held on too tight to lies
about gray and black
and bein' white.

I've seen her spread on my neighbors' bed–
their house the smell of fish sauce
acrid memories of war.
They don't know her story.
She's just a soft blanket, a gift of welcome to
another battleground.

She was a string bikini on the inked up
woman, pulling the hook out of a shark's
mouth, on a South Carolina beach. My kids
said, "Is she a Christian?" There was a cross
tattooed on her leg.

This old rag's been fightin' all her life,
been workin' like hell.
Even the ones who love her
and claim her as their own
call her "blood-stained."

What if she gave up the fight?
Lay out in the sun
on a bed of foxtails.
Let her threads fade into
the soft black earth.

Let Queen Anne's lace and chicory
sprout from her stars, and poppies bloom.
Just lay herself down and rest,
once and for all,
in peace.

Booster Seat Prophet

By Josina Guess

A little voice from the backseat pipes up,
"My teacher said that the guy who killed
Martin Luther King, Jr. died in jail.
She said it was a good thing,
but I don't think so."

At the stop sign,
hands gripping the wheel,
heart slowly thawing, I look away
from the unforgiving pavement, I turn
to look at my child
"Why's that honey? Why isn't it good?"

"Because jail doesn't always heal your heart.
He didn't get a chance for his heart to heal
before he died, and that's what he needed,
so, I'm sad about that."

Starvation

By Jonathan Humanoid

I am fourteen when I first talk about suicidality
My depression wears my skin so well that people call it by my name
We are in the backyard. My step-father and my depression
Empty beer cans clink together on the power saw table

He had said he wanted to talk. This is as close to conversation
as we ever get / the deafening whir of the machine dies and the silence
Becomes a different blade /

Depression taken by the wrist...
Gently presses / single drop of blood
Shows me the difference between horizon and skyline
Teaches me that men must be action and I am a man now
Suggests I either stop being a bitch or do something about it
Tells me he's tired of seeing how this affects my mother
Teaches me about cleanliness so I won't leave another mess for her
Reduces my disease to something comically piteous with his laughter
Releases clumsy flesh with disgust...

Sometimes talking about suicide feels like suffocating on what sustains you
Choking quietly at a table you are told you are not welcomed at
Plate piled high with expression of emotion in men is weakness

I never expected to make it to 20 / carved roadmaps into depression
marking the places, I didn't plan on living long enough to see

I am 24 when I am talking with a friend from Creative Writing
about a girl from class
We are joking about how I like her. Things are going well. I am nervous
My friend makes Shakespearean attempts at wit. Innuendo about
the "deed"
Nay, me fears a much different thing. I am not sure how she will react
to my scars

See, some of my metaphors are not metaphors
When I say that I have bled onto paper
I mean that I know the way crimson splattered against cloud white poem
Feels like unwanted sunrises against half-written skies

There is no silence. Immediate unsheathing of the word dangerous
He decides to tell the girl / blade cuts / we do not talk
about self-destruction!
In the movies, the time-bomb is a secondary villain,
a part of me understands his cutting the single wire to protect her

I am 31 when the internet explodes with news of Robin Williams passing
Awareness buzzes in news stories / Trending promises of being there /
Conversation offered
Society recognizes that we all need to eat to survive / while also
understanding how difficult that is when you have no appetite /
progress is made / mental illness is handled seriously...
A few months later that viral roar becomes a whisper /
conversation stops /

Sometimes talking about suicide is setting out good china for guests
This is reserved for special occasions and it is always about them
Guests will marvel at being included in such a rare occasion
Never asking about the cupboard where the plates are kept

I am 34 when I am sitting around a fire with friends
Grateful (on most days) to have made it to 30, feeling warmth
in the life of the flames as much as I'm warmed by them
they listen to my story and I begin to realize something

Setting the table for dinner has as much to do
with the company as the food

War

By Jonathan Humanoid

My first real, long-term girlfriend is Armenian
I remember lying on her bed
Listening to Against Me! as the eternal cowboy
On vinyl; her head against my chest
Asks if I know the meaning of the word genocide /

Her head against my chest is a needle
I wonder if she can hear my heart skip,
She tells me about the death march; of the cleansing
Her heart is too familiar with this song
She wonders how we can call it a war /

Over the years, I've wondered the same thing, and it still bothers me
How when we're uncomfortable with slaughter we pretty it up
By calling it war /

We treat war like the world is made
Out of construction paper,
Like God is the teacher
Who handed us a pair of scissors
And glue /

We treat invasion
Like we're creating something beautiful
By cutting undesirable pieces
To leave just the ones that fit our vision,
Call it imagination,
Call it destiny,
Act like the teacher has plenty more pieces
To play with...
Just in case we fuck it up beyond appeal /

Sometimes we toss the scraps
And sometimes we find other uses for them
Call them refugees /

I'm watching videos from Aleppo,
Listening to people sing their swan songs,

Accompanied by an orchestra of explosions /

It has been a decade since I last spoke to the woman
Who kissed me with papercut lips, warm with blood
That can be traced back to stains left in the Syrian desert /

It has been a century since
Her people had to redefine a phrase
Had to be flexible with the use of another /

As if home was a debatable term,
That people don't have a right
To remain in the place, they have gifted this word to
On the land where it has been planted and grown from a seed,
As if we can bring a can filled with water
Sprinkle a bit of it
On the fully-grown thing,
someone else has cared for
And suddenly have a right to call it our own /

I'm watching debates on the Syrian crisis
The time is spent debating the term refugee,
A disheartening majority vote to scrap them /

I'm listening, but the needle against my chest
Is playing an old conversation,
A girl who taught me more
Than any revisionist history book ever would,
Is talking about the meaning of the word genocide /

And I'm wondering if we've learned anything /

I hear the fold of construction paper,
The sound the scissors make,
How neatly they cut,
I wonder of the wastebasket we leave the scraps in,
How this has been the metaphor I've used for war
How life cannot be prettied up by changing the words we use /

We don't get another sheet
When we've cut the last sliver from it /

We cannot just empty out the scraps
To make room in the bin for more /

This is real, these people are real,
Human being is not a debatable phrase

Defining What It Means To Be A Man

By Jonathan Humanoid

I just turned 35 and I am wondering if anything I was taught about what it means to be a man was accurate. I think about having sons one day. I promise myself that if I do, they will learn everything that I wish the world had taught me.

My hypothetical future sons will play sports if they want to. If they want to learn ballet I will look up terms on the internet, watch YouTube videos to pick up terminology, proudly shout, "that's my kid, that pirouette was ridiculous!" Right now, that's the only one I know.

If they cry "monster under the bed." They will learn that it's natural to be afraid. They will learn how to love before falling in love. That the friendzone is only as real as the monster under their bed. That expectation is a drawbridge in our chest. Do not keep your heart closed to possibility. Be open to the love that finds you in the form that it does.

They will learn that all of their friends will be bragging about getting laid. How unlikely it is that they actually have. If they want to wait they should. One's interest in sex and how it is expressed is entirely up to them.

They will learn heart break. It is a cinematic cutscene in everyone's main quest. If they hold back their tears I will offer them something to cry about. Playlists that I've made, movies that I have queued up, because it's cathartic and also natural.

I will try to pass down my love for gaming. Introduce them to old friends with gravity defying haircuts, impossibly gargantuan special weapons, and a depth to their ability to display emotion. They will learn the directions on the d-pad. How there is no singular way to be a man. Man up. Man quarter circle forward-punch. Man down for two seconds, up then kick. Man however you want. You are a man.

If my future sons ever question if they are man "enough" Whatever the fuck this means subjectively, I will hold up a mirror. They will learn that this is what a man looks like. If my future sons ever question if that is what they are. I will hold up a mirror. This is who you are. You are you and I love you.

Banana Peel

By Katie Manning

Soon after the news
is repeated across
screens and pages

—my pastor, the father
figure who officiated
our wedding, has been

having sex with a young
woman in our church
for over a year—

I find a banana peel
on the bathroom floor.
Not a whole peel,

just the stem, lying
on the white tile
of a public restroom.

Did someone really
peel a banana while
seated on this toilet?

How could this happen?
Who would do something
so gross? Yet someone

has done this thing.
My disgust doesn't keep
the truth from being true.

A Giant Among Men

By Chris Cambell

She got pregnant before I wanted her to.
My wife felt the pressure of her clock ticking
and made sure she applied that in pleasurable ways.

I hoped it would take a while,
finding solace in stories overheard of couples
spending years rabbiting about,
daily getting lucky but never pregnant,
but that was not our story.

After a few short months
of near daily injections,
off the pill, but never thinking much of it,
we found out.
We even pinpointed the specific day.
I had a bad cold and
was sick for three weeks,
with only one point of entry
to mark the duration.

It's weird knowing
I was knee-deep in a fever dream
the day our son was conceived,
but it's also oddly fitting.

He came unexpectedly early,
behaving in labour as he had in utero.
Having only read two brief chapters of my
manly book on enlisting in the Dad army,
I knew I wasn't ready.

But after 27 hours of labour,
Ezra James Cambell
screamed his lungs dry,
and the entire room was filled
with his enormous cry,
while his delicate body barely
filled my hands.

Left alone with my
premature evacuant
and a cup of milk
too tiny for a doll to drink,
I, fed him first;
he furiously gulped
Every.
Last.
Drop.

Suddenly I realised that
I didn't know how to put him down
and I wasn't even sure if my wife was still alive—
because she'd lost a medieval amount of blood!—
and it had been probably an hour or more since
I'd seen anyone but the other babies in the room around me,
each hooked up to menacing machines
with neverending wires and tubes
unnaturally protruding,
appearing more like experiments or victims,
than children
to my uneducated eye;
their bodies both impossibly small
and unbelievably alien,
made me hold my Ezra close
and cry with unreserved pride
and relief that everyone had said,
"He's so big and strong!
He doesn't belong here at all."

That was when I knew,
no matter how big he'd grow to be,
I would never see anything
but a giant among men.

No River Returns To Its Source, Yet All Rivers Have A Beginning

By Chris Cambell

Growing up, my Mother often said,
"Whatcha mean 'we' white man?"
which I took simply as
another of her embarrassing quirks.

But in the last five years,
those words,
that phrase,
it's come back to haunt me
taking on new life, new meaning,
challenging me to think about my identity.

See, my family history is...unusual.
My father was my grandmother's
younger lover and drug dealer
who offered to marry my Mom
so he could have a 15 year old
live-in cleaner, occasional sex toy,
and punching bag when he was drunk.

The matriarchy betrays itself to the patriarchy
in exchange for convenience and cheap thrills,
leading to the tired cycle of men abusing women;
The oppressor's existence hinges on that of the oppressed.

But, as if that weren't enough,
I am also descended from a long line
of Native Americans, on my mother's side,
and English Pirates, on my father's.
White European men who came to our land uninvited,
have made my mother wish she were dead
so often that she's unsuccessfully attempted suicide
more than anyone else I have ever known;
So either she's ridiculously lucky,
or, she can't do anything right.
I guess it depends on how you look at it.

And though I never really met my father—
he was shot; went from dad to dead
before I was one—
his blood courses through these veins,
(maybe that helps explain the origins of
the hate I held for my mother so long)
and I can never escape that,
no matter how many oceans I cross.

I am both the colonizer and the colonized
wrapped up in a package the color of confusion;
of false recognition followed quickly by disappointment,
unexpectedly drifting in and out of disparate scenes
during a live taping that the actors weren't warned about;
never knowing where my place is,
causing an unidentifiable unease by my mere existence.
I am a sort of self-fulfilling prophecy somebody forgot,
like a wave of lukewarm deja vu
lapping at my own feet,
vaguely familiar but impossible to put a finger on.
Simply self identifying as "Chris"
has never been enough
for things to click
into place.

So when white people say "we"
when talking about me,
in some ways, they're right,
but,
I can't stop myself from thinking,
"Whatcha mean 'we'
white man?"

Immigrant Song 31

By Chris Cambell

I know what it means to burn
all your bridges, to willingly set
your entire past on fire and fan the flames
to further your forward momentum.

But what surprised me,
was how much I missed it,
when it was gone.

Because I quickly learned
immigrant is a four letter word
that automatically makes you wrong.

And when the whole world is
against you, you'll be wishing
there was something—
anything!—
from your old planet,
to which you'd held on.

&then we sit and sorry into each other between talk about the weather

By Keayva Mitchell

Lover, today/this body is still sunken with apologies/a body/s p l i t/from
the body/there are no ready words for *forgiveness*/*of the body*/but
I have spent an entire lifetime trying to pardon/this body/trying to
sabotage/this body/trying to find any/body/to say that my/body/
isn't some city gone wrong/Lover/I have been unfair/I have been going
about this/body/in all the wrong ways/I cannot sorry enough/I cannot
un/lifetime/the day I heave myself into myself/will be a blessing:

> when I am finally dusk cottonfield/
> when this mouth can only laugh
> /too loud/
> when this neck swerves itself into all this
> /sass/when I talk through every movie/
> when my knees resemble your ashtray/
> when I hear/*father*/& don't know
> what/to do with it/
> when a black boy's gunshot wound/rips
> t h r o u g h/ my own chest/
> when I listen to Sade/instead of the
> Britney/I learned to fit in/to you/
> when it takes us an extra two hours/
> to leave because I had to wash/my hair/
> when/this hair/has me crying in
> /frustration/
> /my hair/in ugly twists & a silk scarf
> /to bed/hoping you'll fuck me
> /anyway/

when I am anything/but/glamorous/
when my melanin is everything/but deniable/
when I become every black stereotype you didn't/
even know/I was hiding from/this will be the day/
/Lover/when my/b o d y/
is no longer both the/oak tree/& the chainsaw/
when I tell the lit match of/this body/
//*I will love you despite myself*//
/this body/will be parsed/between/small/prayers/
in the way your hands can never/quite/keep up

&in Palos Verdes we experience the elapsed ache of freedom

By Keayva Mitchell

&he puts the parking brake on/&suddenly my throat is a checkpoint that we cannot pass/my body is all stupid mistake/too brown/&too angry/&besides i want to feign perfect for as long as i can/&it is too late for me to suggest a different trail/&so i let him lead me toward the vulgar sign proclaiming/ Trump National Golf Course/*There's a trail leading down to the ocean*/he promises/&*it's beautiful*/he says/&so i follow/&it is/&for one long stretch i am surrounded by the sea/&a sea of wildflowers/blooming across my hands/winged creatures flutter softly around us/as he cradles my fingers/sugar darling/&winds his way down into the ocean/&i have been writing this poem for ever/&i am beautiful/&intense/&aware of myself/&how when i lift my self to the sky/i can see a gaudy over-sized American flag/snapping me away/&suddenly i can only pay heed the wind wild/jagged/&crisp/ trying to propel me off this land/can't disregard the golf carts heaving through/what might've been an idyllic morning/&he tells me that/ unfortunately/this beauty might not exist without the flashy course/&i remember that in French there is *jolie-laide*/&it is that which is beautiful in its ugliness/&so today i do not argue against what is housed between pretty/&painful/when that man became the president/i admit that for days after i would find myself crying/in restaurants/&in living rooms/&in grocery stores/&in empty bars/&what is the insanity that causes me to ache/over the loss of something this country has never been/&didn't i always know/&hadn't i seen his ugly rear its head into every hard g sound of my life/once a boy spit in my face/&wasn't that our president/&what is he if not a blue-tongued country/spitting in the eyes of its people/&this is not the poem i wanted to write/this pretty-ugly/i would like to escape with the man who stands guard quietly/while i collect enough stones/ to say goodbye to/&who lets me stop every few minutes/&then later will send me ninety-four pictures of everything i call beautiful/i want to tell him that i think i had this exact dream before/without realizing how easily i could've turned to face my nightmare/i want to tell him to breathe a mouthful of pollen into me/but there is a snake loose in this garden/its golden jaw wide/&unhinged/&he never turned me away/but then/i never asked him to/&there is a distinction here/but i don't know if i know it/or care to speak it/&if it'd make much difference anyway//

Iftar: Ramadan In Gaza

By Nancy Johnson James

A photograph.
A family of five sits in a circle surrounded by rubble,
By bombed, bulldozed buildings,
They sit in open air and stones,
And this is still home.

A purple lantern.
Purple tinsel hangs overhead shining against gray.
There are circular dishes, colorful foods, circular bread,
The tires have cooled,
The smoke cleared,
The taste of tear gas washed away.

But the suffering never forget, even when forgotten.
Fast or no fast, bullet or no bullet, god or no god,
The body still craves a life it has never tasted.
The heart wants its home.
People want to move without fear.

I am not Palestinian
Without protest I forget suffering, even my own.
I don't live in Gaza, but I see the stones,
I see the slings and I think of how a David
Has become a Goliath,
And, of how giants fall.

The Gift Of My Hate

By Buddy Wakefield

At the Concert for New York City in Madison Square Garden five weeks
after 9/11 Richard Gere stood in front of millions of viewers and said

*We have the possibility to turn this horrendous energy we are all feeling
from violence and revenge
into compassion into love into understanding.**
The crowd

       booed him

loudly

as if to say,
                   Hey
Buddha Boy,
             We will not be caught dead acting like Jesus Christ.
As if Christ only published concepts he wanted us to
thump instead of experience.

Granted, *compassion* is a wounded word. It gets
banged around in the junk drawer.
It ıs not an entitled driver. Would not survive in California.
Compassion is often the last player picked. So maybe Richard Gere
should have used the word rest to suggest that we curb the poison
of reacting so fast.

But journalists insisted Richard Gere's proposal for love and understanding
was the *wrong time, wrong crowd, wrong message.*
I remember being 27, watching this, feeling
like some fathers do not tell their children *I am proud of you,*
like an entire city had learned the language of a well-disguised suicide
smothered in clever headlines and a swarm of stagy news reporters
who failed to mention that a French man named Antoine Leiris
lost his wife and the mother of his child—
with whom he was madly in love—
to the terrorist attacks in Paris last week.

It was no more excruciating than what happened in Baghdad, in Beirut
or in the West Bank during the same 24 hours.
The difference is that five days later Antoine Leiris was the only man
to post a love letter for his son on the BBC,
an open message to those responsible for killing his wife.
He looked directly into their hungry little pain-bodies and told them
I won't give you the gift of hating you.
Pussy. Pathetic propagandist. Candy-ass liberal.
The insults that followed Antoine's moment of peace made me realize
Love – wounded a word as it may be – can see *all of it*
but *Anger* – anger is only concerned with what it thinks is fair,
narrow like the barrel of the NRA,
like the blueprints to Russia's femininity, to China's childhood,
to North Korea's private parts, to the bruised music of the
Confederate Flag states
still singing like a drunk Englishman in a Tibetan monastery,
loudly, louder, *Hey!*
I'm the Over-Compensator! The Great Annihilator!
Cross me, and you will know my pain!

In each of us
lives a small man
with a
good heart
and an ego the size of
Hitler.
Y'all, why are we not fighting fire with water?
Compassion will not make us lazy.
It is okay to cross these borders. It is okay to stay awake
to love our own ignorance enough to look at it square in the wise guy,
in the bright side, at the parts we are terrified to acknowledge
because of the work it will probably cause us

because there is a chance we have been our own terrorists.
There's a chance we are a failed relationship.
There is a chance that every single day
we are the reason millions of animals actually weep before slaughter
and we do not get to make up for it

by watching adorable YouTube videos
while stuffing our face with their death.

It is more than some sellable cliché
that – through these bodies – we are rooted to the same source,
that we have arrived on this planet to experience form.
Now that we've had some time to do that, please,
let us reintroduce the idea of *questioning everything.*
Excessive packaging. Planned obsolescence. Breeding.
Identity. Fining people
because they didn't have enough money in the first place.
Anything impractical to the eradication of suffering.

Like denying refugees. Like putting a fence around freedom.
Like the oceans of care we keep for this world
getting so landlocked in our chest
that when the answer tries moving over all the God dams built
across our flooded hearts
to surprise us with consciousness
it might look like we are spitting back entitlements at the Earth.
Stay still. Gather your wits. Find their ends. Pull out the slack and say
clearly

Yes.
          Compassion.
Love.
Understanding.

Go ahead. Call me another cliché.
Stick your violence in my meditation.
The worst you can do to me for not joining the gangland war
on Christ's behavior
is shoot me in the look on my face, the one that says *I am not afraid to
understand you. Or to stop you.*

In A New Earth, Eckhart Tolle calls us the noisiest humans in history.
Some things do not need to be fact-checked.
Stop backing up so loudly. You screaming siren on a cell phone.

You heavy-footed upstairs neighbors. Bloated bodies of anger
belting out boos the size of Madison Square Garden
rejecting Richard Gere,
who I know very little about,
but who I suspect, like most humans, is part saint
part fraud, and who reporters had to admit rebounded rather nicely
when he acknowledged what he had to offer was
apparently unpopular right now—

Like taking away your child's assault rifle.
Like the color white.
Like the color brown. Like supporting
the man in Nigeria who found the cure for HIV.
Unpopular is compassion. Like a savings account in Greece.
Like the topic of trafficking Stockholm Syndrome
all the way back from New York City to right here down the West of me

where I am determined to see all of it
because I don't get to go blind again, not without
carving the word *coward* in holy braille on every pen I will ever use
to point out how pain can not digest love. It works the other way.
My body
no longer loves writing poems for mass consumption.
It does not believe in blowing apart.
But I am still right here behind its habits,
stacks of ground down teeth and a mashed-up forehead of rolling credits,
working to see all of it, which I suspect is more productive than giving you

the gift of my hate.

TAKE A STAND

I wish we were all in one big room for this.
Sat around a table larger than
all the problems plaguing us,
groaning under a feast of plates piled high
and drinks that never ran dry.
The evening interrupted
only by our laughter.
Loud. Clear. And pure.
The sort of sound that's impossible
for a body to create until all its
cares have been swept away.

But now is not the time for that.

You're here, at the end of this anthology of poetry, and the easiest thing in the world would be for you to put this down and think to yourself, "That was a nice book." before going about the rest of your day. Lord knows you're busy, you've got other things to do, seemingly infinite distractions all vying for your time and attention.

I'm asking you, begging on bended knees, to resist that urge! If this book moves you to pursue creativity instead of passively accepting injustice for even one hour each month, week, or day, then we will be that much closer to a world where that feast is more than just a dream.

A world where we can triumphantly swap war stories of the blood, sweat, and tears that we splattered across canvases, composition notebooks, and coffee shop open mic stages in our efforts to speak the truth in a telling way. To show people that beauty is more powerful than hate and even in the midst of all the ugly that's thrown at us, there is hope for change.

Yet hope is not gonna come easy or without a fight.

But that's the mission; to fight evil with poetry wherever we find it, no matter the difficulty, no matter the cost. Even when that evil sometimes dares to show its face in our own reflections! None of us are perfect, we don't pretend to be, but we're made strong by our unity of purpose. And we're asking you to join with us, to take a stand in whatever capacity you can.

So it's up to you now! Remember, the world needs much more than just another nice book.

Love + Peace,
Chris Cambell

FIND OUT MORE ABOUT

THESE POETS AT

CHRISTINA BROWN
INSTAGRAM.COM/CHRISTINALEIGHPOETRY

AMAN K. BATRA
AMANKBATRA.COM

VANESSA AYALA
INSTAGRAM.COM/VANESSAYALA

ALEX LUU
INSTAGRAM.COM/ALEXLUUPOETRY

REE BOTTS
INSTAGRAM.COM/REECIOLOGY

MICAH BOURNES
MICAHBOURNES.COM

BETH MAY
INSTAGRAM.COM/HEYBETHMAY

DAHLAK BRATHWAITE
THISISDAHLAK.COM

UMMI TASFIA
INSTAGRAM.COM/TASFIA.WILDPOET

MARK MAZA
INSTAGRAM.COM/MARK.MAZA

ALYSSA MATUCHNIAK
INSTAGRAM.COM/LITTLEMERMAIDLEELEE

ANNE MCCASLIN
INSTAGRAM.COM/BANANOTHY

CARLOS ANDRÉS GÓMEZ
CARLOSLIVE.COM

EMILY JOY
EMILYJOYPOETRY.COM

A. M. SUNBERG
INSTAGRAM.COM/TAKEFLIGHTCHILD

FIND OUT MORE ABOUT

THESE POETS AT

JRAGONFLY JON
INSTAGRAM.COM/JRAGONFLYJON

MALINDA FILLINGIM
FILLINGAM@EC.RR.COM

LAUREN SANDERSON
LAURENSANDERSON.CO

YORAM SYMONS
INSTAGRAM.COM/YORAMTHEPOET

KATELYN DURST
INSTAGRAM.COM/POETKATE

NATASHA HOOPER
THENATASHADEE.COM

AUDREY LANE COCKETT
AUDREYLANE.XYZ

CANDICE EVANS
CANDICEYEVANS@GMAIL.COM

JOSINA GUESS
JOSINASKITCHENTABLE.BLOGSPOT.COM

JONATHAN HUMANOID
INSTAGRAM.COM/JONATHANHUMANOID

KATIE MANNING
KATIEMANNINGPOET.COM

CHRIS CAMBELL
CHRISCAMBELLPOETRY.COM

KEAYVA MITCHELL
INSTAGRAM.COM/KEAYVASAURUS

NANCY JOHNSON JAMES
NANCY.JOHNSON.JAMES@GMAIL.COM

BUDDY WAKEFIELD
BUDDYWAKEFIELD.COM

THIS BOOK BENEFITS THE WORK OF YOUNG CHICAGO AUTHORS

(YOUNGCHICAGOAUTHORS.ORG)

Young Chicago Authors (YCA) have chosen to work with the youth because they believe every young person has an important story to tell. YCA provides young people with the tools, encouragement, and platforms that allow their unique voices to be heard.

Through creative writing, YCA helps young people from all backgrounds to understand the importance of their own stories and those of others, so that they can pursue the path they choose and work to make their communities more just and equitable.

YCA pursues its mission through different types of writing-centered activities that complement one another, including workshops, open mics, performances, and an annual poetry festival, Louder Than A Bomb. Several of these activities take place in YCA's West Town studios, where students gather weekly for free programming.

On any given day, though, YCA's professional teaching artists and associate artists are in schools and other community spaces, working with young people throughout Chicago and the surrounding suburbs. YCA's pedagogy is rooted in Hip Hop culture and expressed in literary forms including poetry and rap.

THIS BOOK BENEFITS THE WORK OF CRITICAL RESISTANCE

(CRITICALRESISTANCE.ORG)

Critical Resistance is building an international grassroots movement to end the Prison Industrial Complex (PIC) by challenging the belief that caging and controlling people makes us safe.

They believe that basic necessities such as food, shelter, and freedom are what really make our communities secure. As such, their work is part of global struggles against inequality and powerlessness.

Critical Resistance's vision is the creation of genuinely healthy and stable communities that respond to harm without relying on imprisonment and punishment. They call this vision "abolition". Drawing, in part, from the legacy of the abolition of slavery in the 1800s. As PIC abolitionists they believe that the prison industrial complex is not a broken system to be fixed.

Rather, the system works precisely as it is designed to—it contains, controls, and kills those people representing the greatest threats to state power. Their goal isn't to improve the system, but to shrink the system into non-existence. They work to build healthy, self-determined communities and promote productive alternatives to the current system.

FIGHT EVIL WITH POETRY

FIND OUT MORE AT
FIGHTEVILWITHPOETRY.COM

CPSIA information can be obtained
at www.ICGtesting.com
Printed in the USA
FSHW011702301118
53913FS